Stephen Bloomfield was a university lecturer for twelve years, teaching masters' level courses in interpretation of accounts and corporate governance. During that ti̶ ̶ ̶ ̶h̶e̶ ̶w̶a̶s̶ ̶a̶ ̶ ̶ ̶ ̶ ̶ ̶ ̶ ̶ ̶ ̶ ̶ ̶ ̶ ̶ ̶ ̶ ̶U̶ universities̶ ̶a̶n̶ ̶s̶ career included ̶b̶e̶ing – among other things – a company ̶ ̶ ̶ ̶ ̶ ̶ ̶or of a major pension fund; an industrial economist and a financial jou̶r̶nalist.

He has written four books: on company rescues; interpreting accounts; raising venture capital – regarded by the Institute of Directors as 'the most authoritative available' at the time of publication; and corporate governance, described by one reviewer as 'required reading for every board director, regulator, MBA student, as well as professionals'.

D0279937

00767040

Also by Stephen Bloomfield

The Small Company Pilot – A Company Survival Guide
Reading Between the Lines of Company Accounts
Venture Capital Funding
Theory and Practice of Corporate Governance

UNDERSTANDING AND INTERPRETING COMPANY ACCOUNTS

Stephen Bloomfield

A How To Book

ROBINSON

ROBINSON

First published in Great Britain in 2016 by Robinson

Copyright © Stephen Bloomfield, 2016

1 3 5 7 9 8 6 4 2

The moral right of the author has been asserted.

All rights reserved.
No part of this publication may be reproduced, stored in a retrieval system, or transmitted, in any form, or by any means, without the prior permission in writing of the publisher, nor be otherwise circulated in any form of binding or cover other than that in which it is published and without a similar condition including this condition being imposed on the subsequent purchaser.

NOTE: The material contained is for general guidance and does not deal with particular circumstances. Laws and regulations are complex and liable to change, and readers should check the current position with relevant authorities or consult appropriate financial advisers before making personal arrangements.

A CIP catalogue record for this book
is available from the British Library.

ISBN 978-1-47213-627-5 (paperback)

Typeset by TW Type, Cornwall
Printed and bound in Great Britain by CPI Group (UK) Ltd, Croydon CR0 4YY
Papers used by Robinson are from well-managed forests and other responsible sources

MIX
Paper from
responsible sources
FSC
www.fsc.org   FSC® C104740

Robinson
is an imprint of
Little, Brown Book Group
Carmelite House
50 Victoria Embankment
London EC4Y 0DZ

An Hachette UK Company
www.hachette.co.uk

www.littlebrown.co.uk

PERTH & KINROSS COUNCIL	
05787040	
Bertrams	12/08/2016
657 SOC	£14.99
STRATH	

How To Books are published by Robinson, an imprint of Little, Brown Book Group.
We welcome proposals from authors who have first-hand experience of their subjects.
Please set out the aims of your book, its target market and its suggested contents in an email to
Nikki.Read@howtobooks.co.uk

Contents

Part Three: Applying

Part Four: Mostly Mischief

Preface and Acknowledgements

This book draws on, develops and extends the content of a previous book – and, I hope, makes some of the techniques of analysis and forecasting clearer. It also draws heavily on the content and techniques from an accounts module I ran, as part of a university MBA course, to help non-specialists understand what accounts show – and what they cannot show.

During my professional career, I had occasion to use accounts on a regular basis. Although trained as an economist, I had little initial familiarity with published accounts and I was thrown in 'at the deep end' when I became a financial journalist and had to make sure I understood what I was writing about.

Later, as a stock-broking analyst and then an investment fund manager (but admittedly with a company secretary's qualification boosting my technical understanding), I found that even what appeared to be quite complicated accounts could reveal large amounts of information to a non-specialist who was prepared to exercise some diligence in breaking the information down and some intelligence in connecting disparate pieces of information together – perhaps derived from other, complementary sources.

When I spent ten years as a 'company doctor' called in to help companies that were experiencing some form of financial or organisational difficulty, I became particularly aware of the nuancing techniques that a skilfully prepared set of accounts could be subjected to. During this time, I encountered many instances of the decline of professional standards among some accounting firms – which often adversely affected the companies to which they were auditors and advisers.

Not being an accountant myself (although I had a professional qualification which at one time allowed the formal audit of company accounts), I was often subjected to an initially condescending attitude from some of the firms whose work I sometimes questioned. Some readers may consequently attribute what they may interpret as critical remarks about accounting concepts – or even accountants – they may find in the text, to a legacy of my interactions with the profession. I had better set the record straight here and state that I really do not hold all the accounting profession in contempt!

I am particularly grateful to Mr Stephen R Jones, company secretary of Rotork plc; Mr Graham Martin, executive director of Tullow Oil plc; Mr Paul Lister, company secretary of Associated British Foods plc; Mr Keith Ruddock, company secretary of Weir Group plc and Mr Philip Hudson Group Company secretary of Drax plc, for granting permission to use information from their published company accounts (not all of which are used or referred to, however). Because of their simplicity and clarity, I have drawn examples mostly from Rotork's 2013 accounts – which is not to say that others are not clear or suitable! I would strongly suggest readers study the equivalent tables in the accounts of other companies as a means of expanding their comprehension and familiarity with published accounts. All those I have listed would be suitable for this.

I am also grateful to the many students from non-technical backgrounds, to whom I lectured over a period of ten years or so on MBA courses – many of whom initially thought numbers were 'hard' and analysing accounts was a task too far – in helping me to develop techniques to try to convince them otherwise. I hope that these techniques will prove to be of use to readers of this book.

Stephen Bloomfield

Introduction

What the book is about

The distinction between *understanding* and *interpreting*

Looking at financial information – the one simple idea

Using contextual information

Structure of the book

Most people could probably quite happily live their lives without needing to know very much about company accounts. But sometimes a basic familiarity with what accounts can reveal about a company can be very important.

Take two examples. For the first, suppose you have a modest nest egg – maybe a few thousand pounds – for emergency use in a 'rainy day'; or possibly, nowadays, a lump sum after losing your job. What are you to do to protect – and possibly enhance – your capital? The current levels of interest offered on the high street are unattractive; for some years Individual Savings Accounts (ISAs) have offered only derisory rates of interest – probably because of the tax-free conditions attached.

As an alternative investment, you might decide to buy little ingots of gold or possibly postage stamps – but neither are very easy to get rid of when you need cash quickly. You could keep your money under the mattress – but that offers no prospect of growth, no interest whatsoever and the possibility of value being eroded by inflation. You could decide to spend your money on consumer goods – but that defeats the purpose of having a nest egg. Or perhaps you might decide to invest it in the stock market.

If you do this you can go to a financial adviser and pay fees for advice (which may or may not be good) and probably buy some form of interest in a 'managed fund', which may or may not meet your expectations depending on how good the advice you were given is and how the economy performs.

As another route to protecting and enhancing your capital, perhaps you decide to invest in shares directly, through the ever-growing number of share-buying 'platforms' offered by banks and brokers.

You can then either pick the companies you want to invest in with a pin from the long lists of companies and funds in the financial pages and take your chances. Or you could do some modest research and probably give yourself a better chance of keeping your capital and even adding to it.

As a second example, suppose you are approaching retirement and may be contemplating how to use your lump sum. From April 2015, which saw the loosening of the regulations for personal pension funds, those who were approaching retirement could choose to withdraw their money (subject to marginal-rate tax charges) and spend it or invest it further as they liked, rather than having to buy an annuity (which had previously been all that was allowed).

For some time prior to the new rules coming into force, newspapers and radio and TV programmes carried (only slightly) tongue-in-cheek stories about the generation of Zimmer-frame wielding Lamborghini owners that would result from the regulation change. Condescending pundits suggested that some eligible savers might be tempted to blow their retirement savings on one big, flashy purchase. In the event, Lamborghini sales did not see a 'silver surge'. Most people are too careful and sensible to splurge nest eggs.

But the basis for the press stories about pensions and the problem with investing nest eggs was the presumption that many financial decisions, taken by people who are not familiar with finance, are poorly justified.

They really are often based only on intuition (which may be misleading); or rumour (which may be mistaken); or simply the advice of others (who may have been lucky once or twice). They can even be based on the shiny, glittery attractions offered by 'opportunities' carefully constructed by people whose principal occupation is cheating others out of their money.

Most people, if they have ever looked at accounts will have balked at both the volume and the apparent impenetrability of the information facing them. They will simply not have known where to make a start, so they don't bother and back a hunch, a poor tip, or a rumour instead. Or they fall for a well-told fairy-tale from a trickster that promises to provide a maximum return for little or no risk.

Hunches, rumour and poor tips are no basis on which to make business or investment decisions.

The prejudice that most people have against the exercise involved in interpreting information shown as numbers is reinforced by the volume of information – both written and numerical – in a set of accounts.

'Numbers' – basic maths, moderate arithmetic, even simple sums – are often thought to be 'hard'. So people shy away from trying to understand the information that accounts represent, thinking that they will be hard too, because they are apparently mostly made up of 'numbers'. Despite their innate caution – the sort of caution which makes them shy away from profligate expenditure like 'investing' in Lamborghinis – they would still rather rely on unscientific and unsuitable investment techniques: their own or friends' hunches or something they might have read in a newspaper written by a journalist who probably really understood only a little more than they do.

The purpose of this book is to demonstrate that accounts are *not* difficult to understand; that basic financial *analysis* is within the grasp of anyone who can understand what simple ratios represent and can perform arithmetic operations that would not tax the computational ability of an averagely able eleven-year-old. And with a bit of perseverance and imagination, most people can make a fair stab at *interpreting* accounts, too.

No formal training in book-keeping is required to analyse a set of company accounts, since there are no technical issues involved. Most adults are already aware of the fundamentals behind profit and loss from their own lives; are well-acquainted with the concept of cash flow and understand the distinction between debt and credit. If you have a nodding acquaintance with these concepts, you are equipped with the basic tools to begin to analyse a set of company accounts.

Interpreting accounts – making sense of the data by applying it to give further information – is the stage beyond simple comprehension of what the figures mean. (And for those who may be puzzled by the distinction between the terms, *information* is what *data* wants to be when it grows up!)

Simply understanding the arithmetic of the accounts and a mechanical application of the analytical techniques described in this book won't be sufficient *by themselves* to enable interpretation of the facts and figures in the accounts, transforming data into something more useful. This requires a bit more imagination than simple analysis – but, again, is well within the capacity of people who are comfortable with understanding the plot of a novel or keeping track of the clues sown in a TV detective series.

Sets of accounts tell a story (or will do if you let them) and it is this story that the process of *interpreting* accounts reveals.

A story usually has to have some context to make it readily comprehensible, so analysing company accounts has to be done in a context – usually against the background of an industry or a particular set of economic conditions. Set against a context it becomes easier to understand what factors affected a company's Profit and Loss account or its cash flow in the period being reviewed, or even to predict the likely effect of conditions it might face in the future.

Extending the story-telling analogy, novels and films have *plots* and *characters* – and so do sets of accounts. The companies are the characters and the plot is revealed by the balance sheet and the Income Statement and Sources and Uses of funds – the context of the company's operations clothes the bare bones of these to make narrative sense.

The end of the narrative of one set of accounts is a bit like one episode in a TV series or a chapter ending in a book. It leads on to what happens next – which is what the analyst is probably really interested in. Using the analytical tools described in this book gives the investigator (since the analyst is like an investigator trying to piece incomplete information together from a variety of sources) the chance to extend the narrative to give some indications of what might happen next.

So, in order to fully understand (that is analyse *and* interpret) a company's narrative, three things are necessary:

1. First, the analyst/investigator has to have an idea of the particular features of an industry that distinguish it from others – these might be things like seasonal demand for products – such as sales of Christmas cards, or dependence on some other economic factor. Sales of kitchen furniture are related to both the level of interest rates and to the numbers of new houses built, for instance. Finding this information is usually not difficult – keeping generally abreast of events, reading commentary on the sector or even the company's own explanations about trading should give an insight into economic conditions.

2. Second, a good run of back data in the form of a series of sets of accounts – three years is usually enough – is needed to provide some comparative information. This is a bit like supporting evidence, in an investigative sense. It provides benchmarks for the behaviour of the company in different conditions.

3. Third, the analyst needs to be able to see the relationships between pieces of information: an idea that an increase in sales might affect a company's need for cash – to fund increased raw materials purchases and more debtors – for instance. This ability to identify consequences comes with practice.

All of this can be distilled into a simple idea:

> *The key to understanding accounts is to see the numbers not as a slab of data but as an organisation of information that represents a strip of time.*

This book is divided into three major parts (three is a magic number in accounts as will be seen at many points in the text) with a tale setting out how accounts can be abused. The three major parts are:

- The first part – *Familiarising* – deals with content of a typical set of accounts from a plc and the fundamental concepts that need to be understood in order to appreciate what accounts are telling

- The second section – *Analysing* – deals with the techniques of analysing the three major components of a set of accounts – the *Balance Sheet* (now sometimes called the *Statement of Assets and Liabilities*); the *Income Statement* (which is the current name for the *Profit and Loss* account); and the *Sources and Uses of Funds* (which is a bit like cash flow).

- The third section – *Applying* – deals with using the information considered in the first two sections in an applied way. Of necessity it requires that some of the tricks that can be used by the unscrupulous to mislead, conceal or distort accounting information are also explained and these are covered in the final section of the book.

TRUE AND FAIR

If you were able to delve beneath the surface of a set of accounts to check every individual ledger, you might find there are quite a large number of innocent mistakes (that probably just happen to cancel each other out) in some of the information that represents the millions of individual transactions that occur in a large company's year.

You might also find that the information used to construct the final numbers is often not fully complete; or that some statements need to be corrected in the light of subsequent information. It also sometimes happens that when a company reports on income and expenses that amount to multi-millions of pounds, an error of a few hundreds of pounds creeps into the final calculations because of mis-keyed numbers or other human error. None of these things is sinister or renders the accounts inaccurate overall – they are sufficiently minor to be considered 'not material' to the outcome for the year as a whole. In other words, in the scale of things they are not going to make much difference to the results seen as a whole.

The final accounts presented for public consumption (either through a stock exchange in the case of a company whose shares can be freely bought and sold; or through the UK registry, Companies House, for private companies) will have been audited according to internationally accepted standards and will carry a statement that the auditors regard them as endorsing the directors' view of them being a 'true and fair' representation of the company's financial situation.

The wording explaining what this means will now stretch over several paragraphs and is usually couched in the negative. In other words, it will principally suggest that the auditors have not found anything that they *need* to report to the shareholders on, from a long list of things that they *might have* reported on.

However, even the most finicky finance director would have to agree that this form of words (designed mostly to protect the auditors from actions from the shareholders over mistakes that they might have made rather than to illuminate the shareholders' understanding) is a blanket term and does *not* mean that they are *completely without fault* or error in the individual details.

What it does mean is that the information can be relied upon to show a fair picture of the company's situation *for the day on which the accounts were prepared and signed off.* And, of course, the day after the accounts were prepared that picture will have altered – since it refers only to the period between the dates specified in the accounts.

EXAMPLES IN THE TEXT

In the first two sections of this book, information taken from the published accounts of UK companies is used to illustrate specific points about the analysis of accounts. These companies, with shares quoted on the London Stock Exchange, are required to produce voluminous sets of highly regulated, scrupulously compiled accounts for the benefit of shareholders and potential shareholders.

Most of the specific examples in this book are taken, with permission, from the accounts of Rotork plc for the financial year 2013. Rotork's accounts are a very good example of the high quality of accounts by UK companies listed on the London Stock Exchange and are admirably suited to instructional purposes because of their clarity and lack of ambiguity.

Occasionally though and, more significantly, accounts are sometimes deliberately constructed to mislead or to conceal the truth – as numerous news-making events over the past two decades or so involving banks, retailers, oil companies and timber companies, have shown.

In this book, specific examples of misleading, distorting and concealing information are mostly taken from the details of operations of a Chinese timber company called Sino-Forest. This company used to be quoted on the Toronto Stock Exchange (where, surprisingly, the state of supervision of companies' behaviour has often left something to be desired). It had an apparently stellar record of profitability but in reality it produced misleading information for nearly twenty years (from 1995 to 2012), which investors allege deliberately concealed its proper financial condition and allowed a few unscrupulous and crooked individuals to make a great deal of money at the expense of less-than-alert sponsoring organisations (while employing some dupes in between to help it do so).

Unfortunately, as the world seems to have become more obsessed with accumulating monetary wealth over the last thirty years or so, the number of dupes seems to have increased and the number of individuals keen to earn their living through duping has also risen. The professional barriers that should have stood up against infractions of honesty and probity seem in many cases to have warped under pressure. In many cases, accountants have been leading the herd in trampling down these barriers – often abandoning professional standards to assist the capacity of their employers to wring the last penny out of employees, customers and organisations, supposedly in the pursuit of economic efficiency and the advancement of 'shareholder interests'.

PART ONE
FAMILIARISING

CHAPTER 1

The Basics: the three main tables and the shape of the accounts

Introduction to the balance sheet – what it is and does

    Ratio analysis

    Internal analysis

    External analysis

Introduction to the Income Statement – what it is and does

Introduction to the Sources and Uses of Funds Statement – what it is and does

Other less valuable components

The crucial importance of the notes

THE BALANCE SHEET – *OR* THE CONSOLIDATED STATEMENT OF THE FINANCIAL POSITION

The balance sheet is the primary document in a set of accounts. Every company has a balance sheet – even though it may never have traded – since it shows the value of the business to the shareholders, at the date it was prepared. This means that a company has a balance sheet *as soon as it is created*. Since every company has a balance sheet from day one of its existence, the balance sheet 'anchors' the rest of the information that collectively forms the accounts.

The balance sheet is now often more formally called the **Consolidated Statement of the Financial Position** – a catchy little title that makes six words do less adequately what two words used to do!

Whatever its name (and balance sheet will be used for brevity and simplicity), it is a *summary* document. It shows the effect on the company's value of the trading undertaken from the very beginning of one year to the end of that same year, by showing the opening and closing book positions for a variety of category of assets and liabilities. Accounts are traditionally 'made up' (made up in the sense of 'compiled' – not 'fabricated'!) for a twelve-month period. The year does not have to be a calendar year and can have a different start date from 1st January. Very occasionally it may be more or less than a strict twelve months, if there are good commercial and legal reasons for doing so. (Where the period in question is longer than twelve months – or shorter – all the components of the accounts have to be made up to the same date).

The balance sheet also shows the net position of all the pluses and minuses of cash and stocks that was necessary to give the company the resources to trade. This is also shown for one year and is shown sometimes (obligatorily for 'listed 'companies; but not necessarily required for private ones) in a table over a period of years, if there is a run of information available.

This means that, over a period of time, the balance sheet accumulates the value of the profits that are retained by the company, adding to them year by year to show a cumulative total. The balance sheet effectively distils and displays information from both the Income Statement (profit or loss) and the cumulative effect of the Sources and Uses of funds, which are the additions or reductions in resources employed by the company. (All these terms and what they mean will be more fully dealt with later).

These attributes mean that with only a modest amount of simple analysis, it allows a perceptive shareholder to make quite sophisticated assessments about the state of current trading, when compared with previous periods.

The balance sheet's real value is often overlooked by the inexperienced, since the attention of shareholders is usually focussed on how much profit a company made in a given trading period – which is shown in the Income Statement (Profit and Loss account). In the short term this often determines the share price of a listed company.

But it would not be unfair to say that the real determinant of long-term value for a company, in the eyes of the market-place, is the strength of its balance sheet. This is because the balance sheet represents the worth of the company or collection of companies that form a group (as will be explained shortly). If the shareholders decided for some reason that they wanted to end the company and break it up, they would all be entitled to a proportionate share in the value of the company, shown by the balance sheet, that their holding of the entire issued shares represented, after the company had settled its debts.

The Profit and Loss account, by contrast, represents only the surplus (or deficit) of income over expenditure incurred in doing whatever the company does – sells Christmas cards, build bridges, run petrol stations – for a specific period of time. That value cannot be apportioned among shareholders.

When examining a balance sheet of a group of companies – most companies with their shares quoted on a stock exchange are in fact groups of companies, with shares being issued in the *holding company* called 'the parent' (of the family) – it is the *group* balance sheet that is of interest. The holding company's balance sheet is usually quite small and has no operational value, in the sense that assets are usually held, for operating purposes, in the *operating subsidiaries* (which are *sister companies* of each other) where the work of undertaking the business gets done.

The group balance sheet consolidates all the individual holdings of assets, liabilities, debtors and creditors into one pool, which represents the overall value of the group (which is of course owned by the shareholders). It is the group value – the collective values of all the subsidiaries – which are of interest in analysing the financial position.

This immediately throws up a problem, given the bulk of the information. How can absolute numbers expressed in pounds (or dollars or euros) be dealt with by the analyst to make sense? This is where the first analytical arithmetical technique comes into its own – the use of simple *ratios*.

Ratios can provide a great deal of information about a company's balance sheet that helps the analyst to compare one company with another or to draw conclusions about how a company's financial position is moving. This goes beyond the simple understanding of how the financial and trading components fit together in any one year and is therefore a *dynamic measure* of a company's position.

Ratio analysis is usually of one or two types.

- *Internal analysis* looks at issues such as the significance of debt or stock holdings in terms of the total value of the balance sheet; or how much time the company gives its creditors to pay, for instance. This can be done for as many years as there is information available.

- *External analysis* looks at the components of the balance sheet (sometimes expressed as ratios) and compares these with other similar companies to give an idea of how well a company is doing in comparison with what may be alternative opportunities to invest.

Both these types of analysis can also be performed over a period of time to give *trend analysis*.

The major balance sheet ratios – how they are constructed; what they measure; and how they can be used – will all be dealt with in Chapter Five.

THE PROFIT AND LOSS ACCOUNT *OR* THE INCOME STATEMENT

Modern usage often tends to favour the term Income Statement (I/S) but older texts may still use Profit and Loss (or P&L). The two are interchangeable for most uses but for consistency from now on income statement will be used, since there are number of concepts – like 'value added' – which sit more comfortably with 'Income Statement'.

The income statement was touched on in the previous chapter. Like the balance sheet, income statement generally run for a twelve-month period which may or may not be a calendar year. They can also, in exceptional circumstances, be for longer or shorter periods. Where the period under review is different from twelve months, then the same period of time must be used for all the components – balance sheet, income statement, sources and uses statement – as was noted before.

The Income Statement shows how the company managed (or not) to add value to the resources of production (land; labour; capital; materials;

entrepreneurship) which it combined to produce its products. This added value is eventually represented by the profit that the company makes. (This is true for *conventional accounts* but not necessarily for different formats – those which show the company's social impact, for instance. These need not concern us further.)

In order for the company to continue to trade successfully, the value added has to be consistently in excess of all the costs of production that the company incurs – for goods bought to provide stock; for wages; taxes; heat, light and power; and so on. For the company to be worth anything to its shareholders, if it is a company with its shares listed on a stock exchange ('a *listed company*'), it has to do more than simply *break even* on its costs; it has to produce a *surplus* which can be paid out as a *dividend*. The dividend is usually expressed as a number of pence per share (including fractions of a penny) and then converted into a *yield* – the dividend is expressed as a percentage of the share price – which enables investors to compare the return on the investment from the shares with alternative investments like bank deposits or investment in property.

Of course, sometimes companies find it impossible to make profits. Temporary deficits, where costs exceed value added, may be absorbed for a little while (and accepted by the stock market) but eventually, if losses continue, the market will determine that the unproductive resources can be better employed elsewhere and the value of shareholdings in chronically loss-making companies will fall to nothing (it is technically possible for the value of collective shareholdings plus reserves to fall to a negative value – but not the value of individual shares). It is also possible for companies to continue to pay a dividend, in certain strictly defined circumstances and for a limited time, even though they may not produce a surplus of value added after costs – in other words, if they make a loss. (To do this they must still have '*available reserves*' – which are strictly defined legally.)

Just as with the balance sheet, both internal and external analysis can be performed using ratios derived from the income statement to give an idea of performance over time – trend analysis – and in comparison with other companies, to see which is the most profitable or efficient (and therefore the more attractive investment).

THE SOURCES AND USES OF FUNDS *OR* CONSOLIDATED CASH FLOW STATEMENT

The Sources and Uses of Funds (S&U) is the third part of the necessary combination of reports that go to make up a set of accounts. It also runs under different names. It is now often called the *consolidated cash flow* – which risks misinterpretation since it does not show *how* cash flows over the company's year (which is what a conventional cash flow does) but only shows how it was *used*, or *where* it went; sometimes it is also called the (even more unwieldy) *consolidated statement of sources and applications of funds*.

Whatever its name in the particular set of accounts, it shows how the company used the money it generated through selling goods and services, disposing of assets or raising capital or bank loans; and how it used that to buy stock, pay dividends, add to its equipment base and perhaps fund extra sales though credit. (Unlike a conventional cash flow – which is often more of a management tool – the Sources and Uses will *not* show the amounts of money that are used to pay labour costs).

The S&U is a bit like a bridge between the Income Statement and the Balance Sheet. It connects the two together – the S&U is constructed from components of both – and it represents the necessary triangular leg that enables an outsider to verify that the Balance Sheet and the Income Statement make sense.

This is an example of the importance of three pieces of information that were alluded to at the start: with three separate, connected pieces of information it is possible to verify the correctness of any of the other two. Without the third piece of connected information, the other two are left hanging in the air with nothing to connect them. Without a S&U, the balance sheet and the income statement could be manipulated to flatter profitability or the company's financial strength and shareholders, creditors and other users of accounts could be deceived. With the S&U in place that is much harder to do (although still not impossible). The number three begins to assert its power!

There is a particular issue which catches some people out when they analyse the numbers in the S&U. What sometimes throws them is the issue of the sums set aside in the income statement for the depreciation of assets. This concept will be dealt with later, but it needs to be flagged now that the S&U and the conventional cash flow have a major conceptual difference. A conventional cash flow deals only with 'real' cash items. By contrast, the S&U adds depreciation back into the company's sources of funds since it is money that the company *extracts itself* to recognise effectively the 'wear-and-tear' costs of each unit of production and so it has to be added back to give a true picture of all the sources.

ADDITIONAL INFORMATION IN PLC ACCOUNTS

In their never-ending quest to try to make the presentation of accounts follow the changed realities of company financing, the accountancy regulatory bodies have continually adjusted accounting terminology.

Changes in terminology

About thirty years ago they decided that the simple presentation of a left-hand/right-hand balance sheet did not reflect the sophistication of companies' financial positions – and what was even worse was that laymen could understand the structure. That would never do. So in the guise of providing more transparency to investors and shareholders, they required companies to provide more information. This also had the useful effect of making the audit fees increase and increasing the accounting jargon – thereby also pushing interpretation possibly further out of the reach of the uninitiated

---

Because of this, plcs often carry lots of additional information in their sets of accounts – not much of which greatly adds to comprehension by outsiders (or insiders, come to that). For the most part, this information can be ignored in a simple analysis. But for the purpose of completeness, the main additional information is described here – and once you have read about it, you can probably forget about it.

THE STATEMENT OF RECOGNISED GAINS AND LOSSES

Plcs with listings (see Appendix Four) also carry some additional
components to these basic ones in their reports The first of these is the
StRGL – the 'struggle'– which shows how assets owned by the company
changed value over the course of the period under consideration.

The need for this is because some companies have large holdings of assets
in other countries that may alter in value due to exchange rate effects, when
their value is translated into one currency for the purposes of the accounts,
as well as because of actual physical additions and disposals.

For some companies this may be significant – their balance sheets may
appear to be strengthened or weakened without them doing anything, or
the movement in value can even run counter to the 'real' trading fortunes of
the company. So it can be misleading not to identify these effects. However,
for the non-specialist, the StRGL's value is limited and no further detailed
consideration will be paid to it in this book.

CONSOLIDATED STATEMENT OF COMPREHENSIVE INCOME

This table shows how the profit earned by the company (after tax is
accounted for) was derived. It often contains very useful information to be
used once the basics of a company or group's operations have been fully
understood. It might, for instance, set out how an apparent reported loss
was actually a combination of a loss from one set of operations (perhaps
now disposed of) and a profit from operations that are still owned.

It will also give details of how currency variations affected the profit –
although usually in an overall way rather than disaggregated by operations,
or by function or by asset. It is a valuable table for sophisticated analysis and
interpretation but probably too tricky to manipulate for basic work.

CONSOLIDATED STATEMENT OF CHANGES IN EQUITY

This table gives the details of changes to the company's capital base during
the year, together with details of payments of dividends to any minority
shareholdings (larger than normal shareholdings that fall between 5 and

24% of the total number of issued shares). It will include the details of any share issues that the company has made; details of any shares held in the company's own treasury; and details of shares issued to employees – including directors – under share ownership or bonus schemes. For most purposes, it is marginally interesting but largely redundant.

THE NOTES TO THE ACCOUNTS – DON'T NEGLECT THESE!

Over the past two decades, the accounts have expanded in volume and content with the inclusion of subordinate tables giving details of comprehensive income, changes in equity; and information about gains and losses that have a material impact on the reported profits and the balance sheet.

In addition to these pieces of information, UK parent companies with subsidiaries with listed bonds – perhaps on a foreign exchange – are required to publish separate accounts for these entities and lodge them with the UK's National Storage Mechanism (NSM) and on their own websites. These can then be used to verify information which the analyst may find useful in building up consolidated forecasts.

These now make explicit (but at the cost of potentially overloading readers with information) much of which had to be dug out by analysts from the fewer (and simpler) tables. This is the result of the accounting bodies trying to balance the competing pressures of transparency and simplicity – but it has been achieved only at the cost of additional volume.

Much of the material now set out in separate tables used to be found in the 'Notes to the accounts'. These are extremely valuable addenda to the main tables that explain the detail of individual entries in the income statement and Balance Sheet. Their value lies in synthesising additional information, derived by putting together the information that they often reveal separately, and to enable what would otherwise be mere conjectures about the company's circumstances to be founded on reliable information.

While the actual accounts only extend to three or four major tables, each occupying about a page or so, the explanatory notes to each category of information may go on for several pages. The individual expansions of information are usually identified with either a superscript numeral or a number in brackets beside the category they go on to give further information about. It is in the multiplicity of these explanatory notes that the nuggets of information about the company – the bits that help so much in *interpreting* the context of the financial position – will be found.

CHAPTER 2

The Balance Sheet – in greater detail

THE SIMPLE STRUCTURE

Once upon a time, when things were much simpler, the balance sheet had two sides that had to match each other – hence the name 'balance sheet'. One side was called 'Assets' (things that the business owns) and the other side was called 'Liabilities' (amounts that the business owes to others). Liabilities included the amount of money subscribed by the shareholders, since it was held that in the event of a liquidation of the company, they might be entitled to this.

In the late 1970s, the left-hand/right-hand presentation was replaced by an up-and-down structure that reclassified some of the categories. The term 'shareholders' funds' was the major category on one side and these were balanced by the 'netted-off' total of assets and liabilities on the other (netting-off means setting the plus and minus values in a category of entries against each other to produce a 'net' value). So some of the categorisations appear to have jumped from one side of the balance sheet to the other. Although it might seem strange, this change supported the contention that the category of shareholders' funds, instead of being a type of liability, was the fundamental of the business. One of the legal conditions surrounding share capital is that it cannot be removed (although in certain circumstances courts may permit this to be done – just as they may compel the payment of dividends in rare circumstances).

The latest format is slightly different again. Now assets are on one 'side' with shareholders' funds and liabilities on the other – a reversion to the idea that the money subscribed by shareholders is an obligation that the company owes. This is a format that nods to the idea of 'shareholder supremacy' but does not fit the rigour of the legal position – that the shareholders' original subscription cannot be removed.

However, these fashions in formatting owe more to current views of corporate governance than to anything else. Whatever the format – old or new – the theoretical position is that shareholders' funds have to balance the net sum of the assets (almost invariably a positive number) and liabilities (a negative number). Normally if the company is trading well, the assets grow faster than the liabilities and the shareholders' funds total reflects this. However, if the company makes a loss or if its *working capital* requirements suddenly expand (perhaps in order to fund more business), then shareholders' funds will suffer (all other things being equal).

Reducing all this information to manageable terms is achieved by using *ratios*. These produce synthetic information by combining one element of the balance sheet in association with another element. While this may sound daunting, no arithmetical skill above being able to manipulate simple fractions is required to do this.

THE NAMING OF PARTS

In looking at the specific components of the balance sheet, some basic descriptions and definitions are in order.

Figure 1 (overleaf) shows the balance sheet of Rotork plc for 2013. Rotork makes flow-control equipment for use in a variety of applications for the oil, gas, power and water industries. It has a balance sheet with most of the components that might be normally encountered; in a conventional (that is, current) format; and with no particularly unusual aspects. (The balance sheet is shown at p. 76 of the report and accounts published by the company – the previous 75 pages are taken up with descriptions of activities and reports from committees of the board.)

The first thing to do is to look at the headings and numbers to get a rough idea of the size of the amounts involved and the 'shape' of the balance sheet – what components bulk particularly large; what is not significant in relation to other components and how the whole thing fits together.

The balance sheet adopts the up-and-down format with assets running down from the top divided into 'non-current' and 'current'. Throughout, the balance sheet notes, listed separately and later, explain the details of each set of numbers.

First on the list are *non-current assets*, which are assets which don't generally move. They include *tangible assets* such as plant, property and equipment; and *intangibles* like goodwill (which represents the premium for control that the company will have paid to buy out other businesses it has acquired); and the value of brands and intellectual property (which are both very difficult to value) and various financial assets including tax credits.

Consolidated balance sheet

At 31 December 2013

	Notes	2013 £000	2012 £000
Non-current assets			
Property, plant and equipment	10	45,871	38,445
Goodwill	11	105,150	80,729
intangible assets	12	53,481	40,743
Derivative financial instruments	23	804	
Deferred tax assets	13	11,778	12,984
Other receivables	15	1,532	1,674
Total non-current assets		218,616	174,575
Current assets			
Inventories	14	75,081	71,100
Trade receivables	15	105,976	95,822
Current tax	15	1,145	1,946
Derivative financial instruments	23	2,933	2,254
Other receivables	15	12,152	9,662
Cash and cash equivalents	16	68,873	59,868
Total current assets		266,160	240,652
Total assets		484,776	415,227
Equity			
Issued equity capital	17	4,344	4,340
Share premium		8,840	8,258
Reserves		6,649	10,356
Retained earnings		312,246	246,369
Total equity		332,079	269,323
Non-current liabilities			
Interest bearing loans and borrowings	19	1,678	116
Employee benefits	20	22,705	32,060
Deferred tax liabilities	13	16,920	13,488
Provisions	21	2,628	2,701
Total non-current liabilities		43,931	48,365
Current liabilities			
Interest bearing loans and borrowings	19	532	56
Trade payables	22	38,019	36,355
Employee benefits	20	17,479	14,065
Current tax	22	14,836	11,143
Derivative financial instruments	23	32	96
Other payables	22	31,002	31,889
Provisions	21	6,866	3,935
Total current liabilities		108,766	97,539
Total liabilities		152,697	145,904
Total equity and liabilities		484,776	415,227

These financial statements were approved by the Board of Directors on 3 March 2014 and were signed on its behalf by: **PI France** and **JM Davis**, Directors.

Figure 1: Rotork's 2013 consolidated balance sheet

A small digression on depreciation . . .

There are few things that neophyte analysts stumble over more than depreciation. It is not a complicated issue but it has the unfortunate characteristic of not appearing in some places (in the balance sheet, for instance) and appearing in others (in the Income Statement, for instance) – both at the same time and depending on the format used. This can give rise to muddle and consequent confusion when the third element of the accounts tripod – the Sources and Uses of Funds Statement – is introduced.

The best way to explain depreciation is to imagine that every item sold takes a tiny bite out of every piece of transport, machinery and office equipment owned by the business as it goes through the production process. All equipment eventually wears out and has to be replaced so the charge for depreciation therefore aligns the gradual wearing out of all the plant owned by the enterprise with the level of production undertaken. If this were not done then the costs of production would be understated. The charge for depreciation helps to properly attribute the economic cost of producing goods to each produced unit.

Depreciation is *not* therefore any of the following:

1. A sinking fund for replacing capital equipment

2. A way of calculating hire purchase charges

3. An inflation-proofing method of calculating replacement costs for plant and machinery

or

4. An indication of how fast a piece of equipment reaches the end of its useful life. (Many pieces of equipment can sometimes go on beyond their fully depreciated life which results in an eventual cash benefit to the company – but some potential under-reporting of 'true' profits).

Lastly and most importantly, depreciation *does not involve the movement of cash*. It is a theoretical concept that involves applying a notional charge to profits, through taking a chunk out of the balance sheet value of assets used in production. The significance of understanding this becomes very important in analysing the sources and uses statement when the mistake is frequently made of not adding back depreciation – and then wondering why the numbers don't make sense . . .

Depreciation *doesn't* appear in the income statement because it is applied to the balance sheet value of the assets. But when the sources and uses statement is reviewed, it will be have to be added back to profits to make sense of the flows.

Conversely, *current assets* are assets which do or can move. They include stocks of raw materials, part-finished goods and goods ready for despatch but not sold; amounts receivable from customers; and cash in hand or at the bank.

Added together, non-current and current assets give a value for *total assets* which has to balance the value of *liabilities and shareholders' interest*, which is the 'other side' of the balance sheet.

SOME DEFINITIONS

Definition 1: *Share Capital*

Share capital is the amount of money subscribed by the owners of the company in order to set it up and allow it to trade. Share capital may be augmented later in the company's life but cannot be reduced – except in very rare circumstances.

Once it is in place, share capital cannot be removed or reduced (unless an equivalent amount is put in place by raising another class of shares of at least equivalent value) except by order of the High Court (in the UK). This is because of the legal presumption that the company is an independent legal entity, different legally from the shareholders; so once the money has been subscribed, *the company* owns the money *not* the shareholders. Taking the money away would be equivalent to theft – almost like murder by strangling the company.

Share capital is also sometimes called *'equity'* (in English/Welsh company law all ordinary shares are equal in value and importance – hence the notion of equivalence). The actual amount of share capital need not be very large (although there are Stock Exchange rules governing how large it has to be for a company whose shares are listed) and it is very important to realise that the value of the share capital in the accounts *bears no relation to the share price of the company.*

Then comes the share premium account.

Definition 2: *Share premium*
When shares are issued to shareholders, they are normally issued at a price in excess of their face value. This is for a variety of reasons, which are not of concern here. But the difference between the nominal share price (the face value) and the actual price at which they are issued is the share premium. This again *bears no relation to the fluctuating daily share price of the company.*

This is followed by reserves and retained earnings.

Definition 3: *Reserves*
Reserves are effectively balancing amounts between the value of assets at the time they were purchased by the company and their current value – since most physical assets will decline in value in time with usage and have to be replaced, reserve sums are usually the excess value of properties and land. *They are not cash amounts* and are not 'liquid' (see Appendix Four).

In accounting terms, assets must be held at the lower of cost and market value in the balance sheet, to satisfy the demands of prudential accounting. But since this would give an equally distorted view of the value of the company if no allowance were made for positive changes in value, revaluation reserves provide a sort of safety valve for the true values to be disclosed.

Definition 4: *Retained earnings*

Retained earnings are one category of reserves. They are the cumulative value of all the profits that have been made by the company after taxation. They are not necessarily a physical amount of money that the company can draw on but signify the surplus that the company has achieved over its lifetime. It used to be the case that industrial businesses would have only a fraction of their retained earnings in cash because so much had been ploughed into the assets that produce the added value by which the company made profits.

The new economy companies – software, design, or other service-based and often light on manufacturing capacity – may well have very large amounts of cash in their retained earnings as they do not have to invest so heavily in physical productive assets.

In old economy companies retained earnings effectively amount to a 'virtual' number that should be added to the company's initial capital base (plus any reserves) to reflect the amounts that the company has been able to add to its asset base.

Definition 5: *Shareholders' funds*

Shareholders' funds are the total of all the above – what the shareholders originally put into the business (which may have been added to over time by further issues of shares) together with all the surpluses that the company has managed to achieve since its incorporation, less the liabilities it owes.

After these come the *liabilities* that the company (or more correctly the group) owes to others. These are, like assets, divided into *non-current and current*.

Non-current liabilities include all the long-term money that the group *owes to bankers and other lenders*. Because Rotork – very unusually in the current age – has a final salary pension scheme (a 'defined benefit' scheme) it also lists *employee benefits* that it knows that it owes. This will be an actuarially calculated figure that extends into the future.

Deferred tax liabilities are calculated on what the group might owe if certain obligations were crystallised. They are recognised but not foreseeably payable (if they were they would become 'current liabilities').

Provisions are the sums that the group has set aside if they have to make payments that cover the cost of contracts not being profitable or for warranties to customers.

Current liabilities include *short-term loans* and *overdrafts; payments to suppliers* taken on credit; *employee benefits* again (falling due in the current year); the *tax* that the company knows that it owes but which it has yet to pay (the Revenue requires payments on set dates) and under the heading '*Other Payables*' the amount that it will pay out to shareholders as *dividends*.

All these lumped together are *total liabilities*. One of the benefits of this presentational format is that there are no *negative numbers*. Equity and liabilities together therefore must equal the value of the assets owned by the group.

DIVIDENDS

One crucial point about a company's reserves has to do with the payment of *dividends*. Even though a company makes a profit it may not pay a dividend unless there are '*available or distributable reserves*' to cover the amount proposed. If dividends were paid out without a reserve in place, it would be a disguised return of capital – which, according to the first definition, is not allowed.

Occasionally the term 'uncovered dividend' is used when company newsletters refer to the payments made by companies. This refers to the amount paid out in dividends being more than the profits earned in the year for which the dividend is being paid. Although this might seem to transgress the disguised return of capital rule, it is permissible provided there are sufficient *distributable reserves* from which to pay.

Most companies aim to have their dividend amount 'covered' at least once by the profits they have earned after taxation. This means that they are only paying out to investor/shareholders what ought to be sustainable. As a result, the amount of dividend cover (expressed as a numerical value) gives an indication of the likely ability of the company to be able to continue to pay dividends at the existing level – a level less than unity means that the dividend may be at risk; more than unity suggest that even if profits dip, then the company might be able to maintain its dividend – which is what investors like.

The distributable reserves would be the level of retained earnings and any *share premium* that might exist. The share premium is not the core capital of the company, of course, but a sum that reflects the amount paid for shares over their face value.

An example of a company paying an uncovered dividend would be the dividend paid by Santander Bank – the dividend in 2014/15 was not covered by the profits made by the bank. The financial statistics in newspapers and online websites will show that the dividend total was only four-fifths covered by the profits made in the year (and this gave a very high yield to an investment in the company – which tended to support the share price).

Companies may sometimes choose to pay an uncovered dividend if there is a sudden reversal in their profits which is very obviously temporary and will be rectified in the next accounting period. Shareholders in publicly listed companies do not like to see dividends being cut and management may conclude it may be worth paying an uncovered dividend to retain a good dividend record (and reduce share price volatility). Santander reduced its dividend half-way through 2014/15 after years of continually increasing payments to shareholders, after a change in management.

A non-definition

The final bit of defining that has to be emphasised, is that *cash and profit are not the same*.

This distinction has too often confused many business owners – and some analysts – much to their eventual cost.

Companies can make losses for a considerable time if they can continue to generate cash – but they will eventually fail. Companies which make profits and do not generate cash, for whatever reason, will also end up on the scrap heap – but more rapidly than through any other way.

Many company managers have been misled into thinking that they must be making profits if they generate cash and so don't bother to review their pricing (and then watch their cash piles gradually diminish). Many owners of what appear to be profitable businesses too often find that they have to go to their backers cap in hand for more equity to support the business – because crucially *the business cannot meet its obligations as they fall due* and is, therefore, insolvent.

The moral is that good ideas that cannot make both cash *and* profits are not good business ideas. For the analyst, this means that a business which relies entirely on other people's money – bankers, trade creditors or other suppliers – needs to be treated very differently in forecasting terms, from one which has no cash. And companies which continually have lots of cash also need to be looked at with some suspicion – but for different reasons, obviously.

THE THREE PRIMARY CHARACTERISTICS OF THE BALANCE SHEET

There are three major characteristics of balance sheets which need to be explored in a little detail.

- First, balance sheets have to balance.

- Second, balance sheets have to be prepared *prudently* – this has implications for the values that are carried into both subsequent years and into others tables.

- Third, the balance sheet has to be *complete*.

The balancing act

All the balance sheets that an analyst will ever see published will do exactly this. So we can almost discard this characteristic were it not for one very important factor – any wonky balance sheet can be *made to balance* by either inventing something to pad out the gap or by leaving something out: for instance, debtors or creditors can be increased or minimised by fiddling with timing or the likelihood of recovery; stock can be flattered or reduced by changing cut-off dates for counting. There are other variations on the same theme, which are dealt with in more detail in the final chapters.

To be meaningful in analytical terms, the balance sheet has to be accompanied by an income statement and a sources and uses of funds statement to enable all the numbers to be verified. These three tables will allow triangulation of the numbers.

Since balance sheets that do not balance are never (formally) published and those that are published by companies with a stock market listing are subject to very stringent regulation, this means that the analyst of a public company's accounts can concentrate on using the triangulation characteristic to help understand the derivation of the individual lines in the accounts – between one table (balance sheet; income statement or sources and uses it doesn't matter) and another. It has to be said that a public company may still fudge the numbers to some extent (and examples of this are given later in Chapters Thirteen and Fourteen), but public company accounts can usually be relied upon to show the overall correct picture. The analyst of a private company's accounts may not be able to take so much on trust.

The triangulation function will help to reveal any peculiarities in the way that the final numbers are composed. It is possible, using this technique, to reveal anomalies *over a period of time* as quirks of the business reveal themselves.

For instance, it is usual to calculate a forecast level of interest charges for a company by applying a realistic projected level of interest to the outstanding level of overdraft and other debt at the end of the year. If done carefully with reasonable assumptions, this should give a reasonably accurate indication of what charges the company might face, if appropriate levels of interest have been chosen.

But what if there has been a substantially higher level of interest charges (taken from the income statement) than the level of overdraft at the end of the last year (taken from the balance sheet) would warrant, when compared with the level of debt at the end of the current year? This suggests that the company uses much more cash during the year than its year-end balance shows. Why should this be the case?

The answer may lie in a number of things – hugely varying stock levels perhaps or wide variations in trading patterns or substantial extension of credit to customers at certain parts of the year. These things may (or may not) indicate variations in trading from the normal which might need to be investigated further. Careful comparison of the three main tables can throw up clues like this.

What the example above illustrates is how one balance sheet by itself (or one income statement or one sources and uses for that matter) is of very little use to the analyst – simply because the relationships which only one balance sheet shows are quite limited and are *not dynamic*.

Prudence – mostly good but not always what it might seem

Accountants are supposed to exercise caution when they compile accounts. They should be prudent. There are not supposed to make any wild guesses as to balance sheet values, but should only use information supported by documentation, receipts and invoices. That is fair enough for most continuing transactions but not quite so simple when applied to looking at assets, for instance. The values of assets that were purchased some time ago are supposed to be reflected in either their scrap value or a realistic resale value – they should be prudent.

However, this inevitably leads to one of two effects. There is the option of either making some subjective valuation (which can be overcome to some extent by employing experts to make valuations) or potentially undervaluing the worth of assets in the zealous pursuit of maintaining a cautious approach that is, in fact, unrealistic. Neither is entirely desirable.

First, experts can often legitimately disagree over valuations. In addition, some experts may be pliable and endorse a valuation suited to a manager's predilections rather than the market's, in the hope of winning repeat business.

Second, undervaluing an asset is of no use to a shareholder who wants to know the accurate value of the company in total. It may occasionally suit a manager to undershoot a valuation since it may make an otherwise asset-fat company look a little leaner to a potential predator (and therefore help the manager keep his job). But it does the shareholder no good at all to have an unrealistically low estimate of the worth of an investment.

Or it may help disguise extravagance. The company jet or the company flat in Mayfair may not look so much of a splurge and stick out so much in the list of assets, while its cost can be hidden in the mass of general capital expenditure that passes through the Income Statement and the Sources and Uses.

This problem bedevils any but the simplest set of accounts and its attempted resolution has led to very damaging outcomes in terms of the rules that have occasionally been applied in the past – particularly when foreign assets have been involved.

The problem of realistic and prudent valuation in the finance sector is more problematic than in others, especially with the rapid development of 'synthetic' financial products that have no easily assessed value until they come to be sold.

To try to overcome the problems, the accounting professions devised and suggested the use of *'mark-to-market' valuations* for some financial instruments. These regulations, embodied in an accounting standard (IFRS 13), required financial assets to be valued at the level at which they could immediately be sold on a market for them – their value should be marked to the market level. The process was supposed to be more or less continual, with the market value being continually revisited, re-assessed if necessary, and revised.

Unfortunately, the process of continual revaluation becomes overwhelming and consequently largely ineffective if there are very many different assets in need of such treatment.

It is also subject to dramatic abuse by the unscrupulous. If no contemporary market exists for a given financial product (for instance, for a very narrowly defined futures contract) then the accountant valuing it is probably theoretically *required* to make one up. And who makes up a market that shows that an asset his employer has bought has no value, or a heavily reduced one (and also keeps his job)?

The problems that result from when well-meaning regulation based on plausible theory meets unscrupulous real world (based often on greed) have been disastrous. They brought about the collapse of Enron in 2001 (which made up its own markets and valued financial products accordingly before it got found out) and also contributed to the financial meltdown of the big banks in 2007–8. The banks had traded lots of 'highly synthetic' products (in other words old financial junk with no certain provenance) between themselves and consequently could not rely on anyone's valuations of them when confidence collapsed.

Completeness – full disclosure

The third essential characteristic of a balance sheet – that of completeness – should be fairly self-evident as a virtue. If a major element of a balance sheet is disregarded or left out through being forgotten, then the balance sheet will either never balance or it will 'balance' but show an inaccurate picture.

The other two legs of the triangle – the Income Statement and the Sources and Uses Statement – enable the outsider to see if all the components have been recorded and included in the balance sheet. While not impossible to fudge all three together, it is exceedingly difficult to do without widespread collusion between managers or complete incompetence by some.

Once again, for the analyst of public companies the essential accuracy and completeness of the balance sheet can be taken as read (although the Tesco case of 2014 – see Chapter Thirteen – is a salutary lesson in how much accounting conventions can be stretched and still not be detected by outsiders for some time). So the triangulation process can be used to explore how the balance sheet has been built up – what proportion of profits has traditionally been put aside as dividend; how the capital spending programme varies year by year; and what happens if there is a variation in profits or cash flow dries temporarily.

A balance sheet should show the 'shape' of the company – whether good or bad: perhaps too much debt; or not enough core capital; possibly over-stocked; or properly funded, cash-rich and with a modern and efficient asset-base. It might even be said that a 'good' balance sheet is a Goldilocks thing: not too much, not too little, just right.

CHAPTER 3

The Income Statement – in greater detail

The importance of the Income Statement

The simple structure

The naming of parts

A small digression on costs . . .

THE IMPORTANCE OF THE INCOME STATEMENT

In some ways the Income Statement attracts more attention than it rightly deserves. In an investment world that is fixated on the short term, the annual and half-yearly releases of the income statement have become the talisman for whether or not a company is 'performing'. In truth, companies that are good investments would show a continual steady and gradual upward movement in profits – a movement definitely in the Goldilocks tendency (not too much, not too little; just right) over a sustained period of time.

The excess of attention though, is because the foremost comparative method of assessing whether a share of a listed company is a good investment or not – the *price/earnings ratio* – is linked indissolubly with the profits earned by a company. Share prices jump or fall on the formal release of this information settling down on more sober examination of the profits reported in combination with the share, structure and health of the balance sheet.

THE SIMPLE STRUCTURE

Figure 2 shows an Income Statement – this one is for Rotork again, because of its simplicity and clarity – from 2013. Like the balance sheet shown in the previous chapter, the sums are shown in thousands of pounds.

Consolidated income statement
For the year ended 31 December 2013

	Notes	2013 £000	2012 £000
Revenue	2	578,440	511,747
Cost of sales		(304,066)	(272,199)
Gross profit		274,374	239,548
Other income	4	206	908
Distribution costs		(5,623)	(4,214)
Administrative expenses		(129,576)	(111,743)
Other expenses	5	(116)	(32)
Adjusted operating profits		151,412	131,866
Amortisation of acquired intangible assets		(12,147)	(7,399)
Operating profit	2	139,265	124,467
Net finance expense	7	(1,268)	(273)
Profit before tax	8	137,997	124,194
Income tax expense	9	(38,488)	(34,879)
Profit for the year		99,509	89,315
Basic earnings per share	18	114.8p	103.1p
Adjusted basic earnings per share	18	124.9p	109.3p
Diluted earnings per share	18	114.3p	102.6p
Adjusted diluted earnings per share	18	124.3p	108.8p

Figure 2: Rotork's 2013 Consolidated Income Statement

THE NAMING OF PARTS

The Income Statement is simpler in format than the balance sheet and maybe has a more straightforward structure for those not familiar with company information. Note also that in the Income Statement – unlike the balance sheet – negative numbers may be employed, signified by the value being in brackets.

At the top of every income statement is the entry headed *revenue*. This is the amount of money that the company (or group) managed to generate through completed sales – *and sales alone* – in the period under consideration. (As notes in the body of the report will go on to explain, this value may be a composite from a variety of currencies if the group trades in different territories.) Companies are required to show the territorial breakdown of their sales and these will usually be dealt with in a note to the main accounts – Note 2 in the accounts of Rotork shows the geographical breakdown. (This is very useful when it comes to trying to forecast the level of sales in subsequent years, since the two general rules in forecasting are – first, disaggregate as much as possible; and second, there can never be too much information to work from. It also indicates the signal importance of looking at the notes to the accounts for amplifying information.)

Beneath this heading will be shown the *cost of sales* – the amounts that were *directly incurred* – in the generation of sales. The cost of sales line is the amount of money spent on *labour and materials* alone to specifically produce the goods that were the subject of the sales – these are the *direct costs of production*.

Subtracting the cost of sales from the revenue gives the *gross profit* – which may also be expressed as the *gross margin*, if it is reduced to a percentage (gross profit divided by turnover).

A SMALL DIGRESSION ON COSTS . . .

While the structure of the income statement may look simpler, on investigation some of the concepts employed can also be confusing to start with. Costs are one area that seems to offer problems to some.

To give an example of how costs are sometimes categorised, they will include the costs of carriage of raw materials *into* the place of production but not the costs of carriage *out of* the place of production, nor the costs of the sales force which won the order(s). Although to a beginner these definitions and distinctions may seem arbitrary, they have a firm foundation in the logic of the production process. What the entrepreneur wants to know is: 'How much did each item sold cost to produce?' and by limiting the calculation of costs to only direct costs of the labour and materials, this can be more easily achieved, with other costs then being controlled in a different way.

2. OPERATING SEGMENTS continued

	Controls 2013	Fluid Systems 2013	Gears 2013	Instruments 2013	Unallocated 2013	Group 2013
Depreciation	4,353	1,692	427	329	–	6,801
Amortisation:						
– Other intangibles	4,363	1,920	403	5,461	–	12,147
– Development costs	1,193	9	12	–	–	1,214
Non-cash items: equity settled share-based payments	881	427	271	35	563	2,177
Net financing expense				–	(1,268)	(1,268)
Acquired as part of business combinations:						
– Goodwill	19,766	3,688	1,398	–	–	24,852
– Intangible assets	19,548	3,277	1,413	–	–	24,238
Capital expenditure	7,108	2,350	581	281	–	10,320

	Controls 2012	Fluid Systems 2012	Gears 2012	Instruments 2012	Unallocated 2012	Group 2012
Depreciation	3,708	1,258	251	235	–	5,452
Amortisation:						
– Other intangibles	733	2,249	218	4,199	–	7,399
– Development costs	924	–	–	–	–	924
Non-cash items: equity settled share-based payments	698	396	271	–	665	2,030
Net financing expense	–	–	–	–	(273)	(273)
Acquired as part of business combinations:						
– Goodwill	–	–	–	13,952	–	13,952
– Intangible assets	–	–	–	9,668	–	9,668
Capital expenditure	8,656	2,113	1,295	372	–	12,436

Balance sheets are reviewed by operating subs diary and operating segment balance sheets are not prepared, as such no further analysis of operating segments assets and liabilities are presented.

Geographical analysis:

	UK 2013	Rest of Europe 2013	USA 2013	Other Americas 2013	Rest of World 2013	Group 2013
Revenue from external customers by location of customer	31,765	180,865	117,346	59,112	189,352	578,440
Non-current assets:						
– Goodwill	5,691	55,205	40,154	770	3,330	105,150
– Intangible assets	5,538	27,317	20,351		275	53,481
– Property, plant and equipment	16,304	15,176	6,706	768	6,917	45,871

	UK 2012	Rest of Europe 2012	USA 2012	Other Americas 2012	Rest of World 2012	Group 2012
Revenue from external customers by location of customer	28,448	156,525	106,027	53,323	167,424	511,747
Non-current assets:						
– Goodwill	5,009	31,925	39,603	776	3,416	80,729
– Intangible assets	4,496	11,107	24,288	506	346	40,743
– Property, plant and equipment	13,914	10,529	6,005	622	7,345	38,445

Figure 3: Note 2 Rotork's geographical breakdown of income

(There is, of course, nothing to stop individual enterprises refining and extending their calculations of what sales cost according to their own definitions. What is being discussed here is the common format for published accounts.)

After the gross profit line comes *other income*. In the Rotork accounts, Note 4 explains that this is the excess over book costs that the disposal of plant and property made. Most companies will routinely make slightly more on the disposal of their assets (in the normal course of up-dating and realigning their asset base) than the value held in the books – and this is what the *other income* line (usually) represents.

Distribution costs are what it costs the group to get its sales into customers' hands; *administration costs* are what it costs to run all the parts of the organisation which support the main activity – office costs; marketing; legal; accounting; personnel costs and so on.

Other expenses will normally include any losses made on disposal – the opposite to the effect noted above where an asset could only be sold below its depreciated value.

In Rotork's case, there is also a line headed 'Amortisation of Acquired Intangible Assets'. This rather forbidding-sounding line is the amount that the company has to write off each year attributable to the acquisitions it has made.

These amounts have to be written off because they are in excess of the tangible value of the acquisitions. This happens because in order to prise a successful company out of the grip of its existing shareholders, a price usually has to be paid above the verifiable value of the assets in that business. This is called *the premium for control*. The premium can't be allowed to stay in the Balance Sheet – because that would offend the prudence rule – so it has to be written off.

The conventions of Balance Sheet accounting mean that for the protection of shareholders and creditors only prudent, verifiable values can be included in Balance Sheet amounts. The premium for control immediately poses a problem: it is undeniably *unverifiable* as an asset value (because it was subject to negotiation between buyer and seller) so it can't go in the Balance Sheet.

The solution is to write it off 'through' the Income Statement over a period of years – just like writing off depreciation through the balance sheet adjustments made to tangible assets.

After all these costs have been taken into account, what is left is *operating profit*. This is therefore equivalent to the 'clean' profit that the company can achieve without paying out money for goods and services. It is the profit from operations as if they were *clean of the financing costs* that are involved in funding the business.

Once these are taken into account – in the line headed *net finance expenses* – what is left is the profit the company has achieved before it is subject to tax, or in other words – the *pre-tax profit*.

Net finance expenses are the charge, or sometimes credit, to operating profit that has to be made as a result of the impact of financing the business. If the company has to borrow more than it has in cash then the net finance expense will be a charge; if it has more cash than debt then there will be a credit to the income statement. The same result can also occur, of course, if the rate of interest paid on (modest) debt balances is much greater than the interest paid on large cash balances . . . so care has to be taken in making snap judgements about the composition of the balance sheet (and the effect on the income statement) without an examination of *all* the accounting information.

Interest charges and tax . . .

As an aside, from the paragraph above, it can be seen that interest charges are usually an allowable expense against profit before tax is assessed.

This has resulted in the development of so-called 'financial engineering' in some large companies – those funded by private backers (without a listing on a stock exchange). These companies' balance sheets are heavily loaded with debt (loaned by the company's backers who then receive income in interest payments) and consequently the companies have to pay no (or very little) tax.

This doesn't happen in listed companies, first, because shareholders would be very uneasy about the huge levels of debt involved and, second, because it only works if the funding can be provided by the company's backers (who then effectively benefit twice – through interest payments and through any dividends they may receive).

The pre-tax profit figure is the headline figure that often prompts changes in the share price of companies when reported. But what is really moving the share price is the number in the next line – basic *earnings per share* (or one of its variants involving some adjustments which are identified in the notes to the accounts).

The earnings per share value is the amount of profit (after tax) earned by the company in the accounting period which is attributable to each share (in other words the earnings divided by all the shares in issue and owned by shareholders). When this is divided into the price that the company's shares are trading at it gives a ratio – the *Price/Earnings ratio* or, more simply, *PE*.

Essentially the PE ratio gives a value for how many years it would take the earnings generated by the company to account for the share price. There is no absolute comparative benchmark value for this but all other things being equal, a PE of, say. 4.6 is better (cheaper) than one of, say, 21.0.

But life is never that simple and the PE can really only provide a useful measure of value when taken in context. This contextual evaluation should be in two dimensions – longitudinally (that is, over a span of time relating to both the history and projected value of the measure for a single company) and horizontally in comparison both with other companies and a composite value which aggregates all the individual PEs of companies that are available and is known as 'the market PE'. These measures will be examined at length in a later chapter.

Exceptional and Extraordinary Costs

These two terms don't appear in the Rotork accounts for 2013 but they may be encountered when looking at other companies or in other years.

Notes to the Group financial statements continued

For the year ended 31 December 2013

18. EARNINGS PER SHARE

Basic earnings per share

Earnings per share is calculated for both the current and previous years using the profit attributable to the ordinary shareholders for the year. The earnings per share calculation is based on 86.7m shares (2012: 86.6m shares) being the weighted average number of ordinary shares in issue (net of own ordinary shares held) for the year.

	2013	2012
Net profit attributable to ordinary shareholders	**99,509**	89,315
Weighted average number of ordinary shares		
Issued ordinary shares at 1 January	**86,638**	86,523
Effect of own shares held	**44**	55
Effect of shares issued under Share option schemes/Sharesave plans	**9**	14
Weighted average number of ordinary shares during the year	**86,691**	86,592
Basic earnings per share	**114.8p**	103.1p

Adjusted basic earnings per share

Adjusted basic earnings per share is calculated for both the current and previous years using the profit attributable to the ordinary shareholders for the year after adding back the after tax amortisation charge.

	2013	2012
Net profit attributable to ordinary shareholders	**99,509**	89,315
Amortisation	**12,147**	7,399
Tax effect on amortisation at effective rate	**(3,388)**	(2,078)
Adjusted net profit attributable to ordinary shareholders	**108,268**	94,636
Weighted average number of ordinary shares during the year	**86,691**	86,592
Adjusted basic earnings per share	**124.9p**	109.3p

Diluted earnings per share

Diluted earnings per share is based on the profit for the year attributable to the ordinary shareholders and 87.1m shares (2012: 87.0m shares). The number of shares is equal to the weighted average number of ordinary shares in issue (net of own ordinary shares held) adjusted to assume conversion of all potentially dilutive ordinary shares. The Company has three categories of potentially dilutive ordinary shares: those share options granted to employees under the Share option scheme and Sharesave plan where the exercise price is less than the average market price of the Company's ordinary shares during the year and contingently issuable shares awarded under the Long Term Incentive Plan (LTIP).

	2013	2012
Net profit attributable to ordinary shareholders	**99,509**	89,315
Weighted average number of ordinary shares (diluted)		
Weighted average number of ordinary shares for the year	**86,691**	86,592
Effect of Sharesave options in issue	**103**	106
Effect of LTIP shares in issue	**277**	343
Weighted average number of ordinary shares (diluted) during the year	**87,071**	87,041
Diluted earnings per share	**114.3p**	102.6p
Adjusted diluted earnings per share	**124.3p**	108.8p

Figure 4: Adjustments to earnings Note 18

Exceptional costs are costs which might occur in trading but are not part of the normally expected run of events. They might involve the costs of closing a factory or an office for instance – which might be expected to happen at some time and is not so unusual that it warrants being termed *extraordinary* – these are a type of costs that are so unusual that they are outside the normal course of trading events. Extraordinary events might include perhaps the disruption caused by a fire at a factory or some other event that could not reasonably be expected to occur.

Because of this – the issue of reasonable expectation – exceptional charges are taken 'above the line' in reporting pre-tax income. They are disruptive but not so unusual that companies cannot expect to encounter them. They are included in the trend of earnings in consequence.

By contrast, extraordinary costs – very unusual events that would interfere with understanding the company's financial record – are taken outside the run of earnings and are therefore referred to as being 'below the line' – the pre-tax line.

The PE is a means of putting all the different levels of profits earned by different companies on a comparable basis so that investors can determine which are good investments – which are cheap; which are fairly priced and which are expensive. (It is a prime example of the ability of ratios to make disparate information comparable. Much more use of this technique will be examined in subsequent chapters).

The comparison is not infallible and it has to be tempered with some contextual knowledge – but it is the basis for evaluation on which investment decision-making rests.

CHAPTER 4

The Sources and Uses of funds – in greater detail

The simple structure

The purpose of the S&U

The naming of parts

What the S&U represents

THE SIMPLE STRUCTURE

There are no new definitions to be introduced for the S&U. Since it is a composite statement which links the balance sheet and income statement, it cannot have any new items.

The only additional element that has not been seen before at any great length is the amount that the company charges for depreciation; the rationale behind this was covered in the box on pages 17–18.

The S&U synthesises information from combining the income statement and the balance sheet and provides more information out of this synthesis. Strictly speaking, although it is sometimes referred to in some accounts as a 'cash-flow statement', it is not that at all, since it includes the non-cash item of depreciation. (Rotork's accounts which have been used to illustrate concepts comes close to doing this but just avoids terminological confusion by saying that it is a 'consolidated statement of cash flows' – which, of course is different from a [single] cash-flow.)

No new names then – but it still makes sense to go through a typical S&U: Rotork's is used again to see how a typical S&U is constructed.

THE PURPOSE OF THE S&U

The primary purpose of the S&U is to show where the money that came into a company came from and where it went to. The Rotork table shows this by activity – operations; investment; and financing – so although it looks confusing at first, it is really quite straightforward.

Whatever the format, the S&U takes the money generated from sales and adds back the depreciation that the company imposed on itself (re-read the rationale for this again if you are unclear why it should be so), stirs in the funding from additions to the equity base; and then shows how the company spent that total sum on plant and equipment, dividends, tax and *working capital* (see below).

THE NAMING OF PARTS

Rotork's accounts helpfully break down activities into the three components – operations; investment and financing – listed above. This means that the company is producing – almost – three mini-S&U statements which represent flows from each of the elements of its business.

That being the case, then the money paid in interest which contributed to pre-tax profits has to be shown separately – as does any money received from deposits, by making appropriate adjustments in the categories of activity covered by the mini-S&Us.

Looking at the Rotork table in detail, the first component of the flows is that accounted for by operations – those activities that the company was set up to undertake. The first of these on the inflows side is the profit (or loss) made by the business in the period under consideration.

After that the accounts show the amounts of money that are written off the profit for the depreciation of intangible assets held by the company. These might be patent rights and other intellectual property for instance; or the value attributed to a particular brand name; or most likely, the 'premium

Consolidated statement cash flows
For the year ended 31 December 2013

	None	2013 £000	2013 £000	2012 £000	2012 £000
Cash flows from operating activities					
Profit for the year		**99,509**		89,315	
Adjustments for:					
Amortisation of intangibles		**12,147**		7,399	
Amortisation of development costs		**1,214**		924	
Depreciation		**6,801**		5,452	
Equity settled share-based payment expense		**2,178**		2,030	
Profit on sale of property, plant and equipment		**(25)**		(859)	
Net finance expense		**1,268**		273	
Income tax expense		**38,488**		34,879	
		161,580		139,413	
Increase in inventories		**(1,740)**		(9,474)	
Increase in trade and other receivables		**(10,786)**		(22,201)	
Decrease in trade and other payables		**(1,778)**		(3,341)	
Difference between pension charge and cash contribution		**(534)**		(7,211)	
Increase/(decrease) in provisions		**863**		(264)	
Increase in other employee benefits		**2,621**		1,711	
		150,226		118,614	
Income taxes paid		**(39,866)**		(37,641)	
Cash flows from operating activities			**40,360**		
Investing activities					
Purchase of property, plant and equipment		**(10,419)**		(12,564)	
Development costs capitalised		**(2,033)**		(2,075)	
Sale of property, plant and equipment		**159**		1,007	
Acquisition of businesses, net of cash acquired	3	**(43,235)**		(20,674)	
Contingent consideration paid		**(250)**		(200)	
Interest received		**917**		623	
Cash flows from investing activities			**54,861**		80,973
Issue of ordinary share capital		**586**		425	
Purchase of ordinary share capital		**(5,601)**		(2,850)	
Interest paid		**(653)**		(163)	
Prepayment of amounts borrowed		**(618)**		(64)	
Prepayment of finance lease liabilities		**(34)**		(68)	
Dividends paid on ordinary shares		**(38,735)**		(33,924)	
Cash flows from financing activities			**(45,055)**		(36,644)
Increase in cash and cash equivalents			**10,444**		10,446
Cash and cash equivalents at 1 January			**59,868**		48,519
Effect of exchange rate fluctuations on cash held			**(1,439)**		903
Cash and cash equivalents at 31 December	16		**68,873**		59,868

Figure 5: Rotork's 2013 S&U – 'The Consolidated Statement of Cash Flows'

for control' that had to be paid to the owners of a business bought by the company. This 'goodwill' value has to be written off just like the value of physical assets.

Any assets sales that the company has undertaken represent an inflow and will appear on the inflow side – but only if the sale value was for *less* than the fully depreciated value. Similarly, if the sale was achieved at a price *higher* than the fully depreciated value then that amount has to be *taken off* the inflow.

This is counter-intuitive and these adjustments look odd at first. However, if they are thought of as adjustments to depreciation then the rationale becomes clearer. At root, the S&U is about showing core flows of cash – so changes in the value of assets sold have to be reflected also against how much depreciation has already been charged against them. If they are sold for more than their book value then depreciation has been under-charged and an adjusting amount has to be included; if for less, then it has been over-charged and vice versa.

On the Rotork S&U there is an entry for *net finance expense*, which falls in the operating activities section. This is a recognition that the company has had to employ money from banks and credit houses to operate and so it legitimately falls in this section. The money it earns on its own balances are not considered to be part of core operations and are shown in 'Inflows from investing activities'.

The items that follow – *income tax expense* – is heavily affected by the timing of payments to the authorities on corporation tax, some VAT payments (which may not be 'off-settable' against other payments) and payments made on shareholders' dividends (National Insurance payments, although a tax, are regarded as one of the costs of employment and are not shown separately). For various technical reasons which are beyond the scope of this text, the amount of tax expense in 'operating activities inflow' is usually fairly static in most companies.

The Rotork accounts then show three items collectively known as *working capital*.

The working capital of the company is the amount of money in total devoted to spending on 1) stock 2) payables and 3) receivables. If it is shown as an aggregated sum for 'working capital' it may well be a 'netted-off' amount; the movements in the three components listed are not usually in the same direction so there will be negative and positive numbers mixed up in the overall sum.

Money spent on stock is usually an *outflow* from the company's coffers; money spent on expanding sales by giving credit to customers (either as device specifically to encourage sales or as consequence of expanded sales, which has the effect of expanding receivables) is also usually an *outflow* from the company; and money drawn in from customers paying off their accounts with the company is usually an *inflow*.

'Usually' is in quotation marks because all these can change direction from year to year and be either positive or negative in any one year. For instance, if the company decides to run down stocks, money *not* spent on that can be shown as a positive number since it represents the amounts consumed from the level of stocks accumulated from past expenditure periods (so it is negative spending). If the company gives less credit to customers (for a variety of reasons), then it may also be able to reduce the amounts by which it has funded its customers' sales and so produce an effective inflow of cash. If it is called upon to pay its debts more promptly then it may have to spend more cash in a given time period on the same level of stock purchases – an outflow.

Current accounting doctrine prefers that the individual sums should be shown without being netted-off where possible, to try to make all this clearer.

Although these don't appear in the Rotork accounts (for the 2013 financial year), if there are *extraordinary* items in the income statement then these will have to be added back (if they are charged as debits); or taken away, if they are unusual credits. *Exceptional* items will already have been taken account of in arriving at the pre-tax figure so they don't figure in the cash flow.

The other entries in the various categories are all self-explanatory and their provenance should be obvious.

WHAT THE S&U REPRESENTS

The primary physical characteristic of the S&U, like the balance sheet, is *it has to balance.*

Money going out of the company has to balance what has come in. The company cannot spend money that isn't there any more than anyone else – with the possible exception of the government and banks (both of which can create money). However, while the statement that the company can't spend money that isn't there is absolutely true, it is also technically avoidable for limited periods if the company spends other people's money, by using such techniques as taking extended credit for purchases.

So the S&U shows as a final sum the additional money that the company may have had to raise from banks in the form of loans *or* an increase in the cash that is generated from operations and used to reduce its own debts (or swell its cash balances). What the company can also do, of course, is run down its cash balances (if it has them) and consume resources that it accumulated from previous surpluses if it needs to, rather than go to a bank for more money or tap its shareholders for additional funding.

Sometimes – unusually – it is possible to see companies both increasing their cash balances *and* taking on more debt. This may be the case where local trading conditions, or the timing of investments, make it advantageous to prefer debt over the use of cash.

Most of the cash that a business normally generates comes from sales, so the 'outcome' of the income statement is usually the source of most of the company's funding. The S&U is a bit like the drive train of a clock: just like the drive train transfers the energy of the clock's mechanism to the clock's face to show the time, so the S&U shows how the balance sheet was altered by a consequence of all the company's energy in making sales. It converts movements in profit into movements in cash or cash-bought assets.

In the case of the accounts prepared by Rotork which have been taken as an example, it may look to the casual eye that the S&U doesn't balance – the format adopted doesn't appear to show two identical numbers. But if all the flows from all the various activities – operations; investing; and finance— are added together, then the resulting picture is like this:

Net flows from operations	110360m
Net flows from investing	(54861m)
Net flows from financing	(45055m)
To give a net positive value of	10444m

Which is the number by which cash balances have risen (after taking into account exchange rate fluctuations of £1439m).

The S&U has shown how the company spent the money it managed to generate or borrow over the year. The general rule of understanding and interpreting accounts applies strongly in the case of the S&U. Looking at one S&U by itself means much less than taking a view over two, or even three – when trends become much more apparent. There are, of course, two sets already available, since every set of accounts carries the previous year's figures to enable a modest comparison to be made. So an additional set of accounts will give a third year to look at.

The trends revealed by the S&U are prime elements in any predictions that might be made about a company's future trading.

PART TWO

ANALYSING

CHAPTER 5

Exploding and exploring the Balance Sheet

Individual elements explained in detail

A very simple piece of analysis

The major ratios

    Financial

    Liquidity

    Working capital

INDIVIDUAL ELEMENTS EXPLAINED IN DETAIL

Familiarity with the elements that constitute a balance sheet and the terms that apply to them, opens up the possibility of looking at the shape and structure of the company's finances, to permit comparisons with other years and with other similar businesses. This can then give clues to the way that the company is affected by operational events and what might happen to profits, cash flow and the strength of the company's finances in subsequent years. This will then help the analyst to evaluate the potential of an investment in the company under examination.

The individual components of the balance sheet will, of course, tell a great deal about the structure of a company at any given point. Most of the valuable insights are not revealed in looking at individual elements in isolation but in using them in combination with other information to give ratios and proportions which can then give the analyst a better indication (relative values rather than absolutes and in comparison with past information) about trends.

A VERY SIMPLE PIECE OF ANALYSIS

As a very simple example using the information contained in Rotork's 2013 accounts again – the total level of debt that the company had at the close of its year was £2.2m (£1,678,000 in long-term interest-bearing loans and borrowings; £532,000 in short-term loans and borrowings).

While that sum, in absolute terms, is enough to allow a couple of people a fairly good weekend in Brighton, it doesn't really say much about what it means to Rotork. It could be crippling; it could be insignificant and persistent; or it could be a mere temporary dip into debt that is eradicated very soon. In short it is very interesting in combination with other detail – but largely useless by itself.

Only when the level of debt is compared against the level of cash that the company has in its various bank accounts or with third party accounts – £72.610m (in cash, cash equivalents and derivative financial instruments) – can it be seen that Rotork really had only insignificant amounts of debt *at the year-end, when the accounts were made up to.* As a proportion of its total balance sheet value – £484.776m – the debt was insignificant.

That simple comparison – looking at what the value of one component of the balance sheet was at the time that accounts were made up to and then comparing it with another relevant figure to provide insight into the company's position – is pretty much all that analysing a balance sheet is about. This simple comparison has given a good deal of information that can then be worked on further (as will be seen in Chapters Eight, Nine and Ten) to provide more useful information that can be employed in forecasting and evaluating. More information from other comparisons will, of course, provide a rounded picture. Just like making up a jigsaw, the whole image really only becomes intelligible when lots of individual pieces are added together to produce a recognisable whole.

While this may seem initially daunting, a great deal of valuable information can be obtained by manipulating figures with a requirement for no more facility with numbers than could be expected of a reasonably able eleven-year-old.

THE MAJOR RATIOS

Although the range of potential comparisons that are meaningful is extensive, there are really only three major categories of ratio that are most commonly employed in analysing the balance sheet:

1. **Financial ratios**: these include

    *   *gearing* – or to use the currently more fashionable American term, *leverage* – which is the ratio of debt to total assets employed by the business (in reality gearing and leverage when correctly used are two different things);

    *   *liquidity ratios* – how much of the balance sheet is in easily realisable form; there are two of these:

        *   the *current ratio* – current total assets divided by current total liabilities

        *   its close cousin, *the quick ratio* or *'acid test'* – which shows how quickly a company could convert realisable assets into cash if it had to.

2. **Working capital ratios** – these involve looking at

    *   *debtor-* and *creditor-days*, which are the lengths of time that the company takes to pay its debts to suppliers and the amount of time it takes to collect money from customers respectively;

    *   the *stock-turn* – the amount of times stock is turned over during a year.

3. **The Net Asset Value** (per share).

The *financial ratios* are all to do with cash in one form or another.

Gearing is not a consistently defined value in analysis unfortunately, but (however defined) its purpose is to show the effect of using other people's money to run a business.

It can be defined as *either*

- the total of debt (less cash) divided by the total assets (including both debt and cash) employed by the company

or

- all debt (less all cash) divided by shareholders' equity.

Of these two, the former is the more useful and more common since it shows the full effects of debt taking into account all the financial components that make up the business. The second entity is more correctly known as the 'debt/equity ratio' and shows in truth a slightly different concept – how much shareholders' entitlements are likely to outweigh or be swamped by other obligations to other funding parties.

In times of low interest rates when the repayment terms are usually low, it makes a lot of sense managerially to run a business using someone else's cash. (Perversely this can also happen when inflation is very high and creditors can be paid back in fixed sums of steadily diminishing value). This is, of course, provided that the returns from so doing outweigh the costs of repayments to be made on the capital provided by others – banks, loan companies, trade finance houses and so on (which is, of course, when interest rates are low).

When the costs of repaying interest charges are high, though, this strategy can work against a company. The returns from trading may be outweighed by higher interest charges on a constant level of debt if interest rates rise. An astute management will try to balance its use of debt (however constituted) against the prevailing economic conditions, if it can, increasing its use of debt in easy times and reducing debt in hard times. (As an aside, this is in contradiction to the directions in which the public finances should be run.)

Sometimes, of course, companies are forced to increase debt when they suffer some form of trading reversal and this may run counter to the 'normal' pattern of reducing debt when times get hard. Such movements then make it even more difficult for the company to recover since it has to push harder against the problems that caused the increase in debt *and* the effect of higher interest payments, both of which will tend to the continuation of the erosion of pre-tax profits.

The Liquidity Ratios

There are two of these.

1. The *current ratio* is a broad indication of a company's short-term financial position. It is expressed in the form

   current assets/current liabilities

   to give a numerical value.

   If the value of the expression is greater than 1 then the company (nominally) has a surplus of assets over liabilities. However, a value of 2 would be the minimum considered prudent for credit-worthiness because not all assets are readily exchangeable for cash and even if they are, then the company may not be able to continue in business with all its stock gone.

2. The *quick ratio* attempts to get round this problem by removing stocks from the value of current assets. It has the form:

   (current assets – stock)/current liabilities

   This then indicates what would happen if the company had to settle up with its creditors as soon as possible. The quick ratio is sometimes called the *acid test* in consequence, since it represents an extreme case.

If the acid test produces a dividend value of less than 1 it *may* indicate possible problems. Some companies though – supermarkets, for instance – often have terms of trade which allow them to sell their stocks before they pay their suppliers. This means that they can operate with very low quick ratios – sometimes as low as 0.2.

Obviously, then, and once more, context is everything and the best use of the quick ratio is as a longitudinal trend indicator, to show whether the company's position is improving or deteriorating over time (but even this is subject to qualifications, especially depending on the starting point).

Working capital ratios

The working capital ratios, despite originating in balance sheet values, could be regarded as being closer in their concepts to the operational ratios that are derived from the Income Statement.

They show how a company's operations affect its financial structure at root. Financial ratios are usually the consequence of operations (at least after a few years of trading) and so the way that the working capital ratios develop – since they involve the 'feedstock' of the company's activities – are (usually) leading factors in the change in the balance sheet's structure.

In simple analysis there are three ratios of importance – these are the *debtor days' ratio*; the *creditor days' ratio*; and the *stock turn*.

The debtor days' ratio is now more usually called the *debt collection period*. The company's debtors are the customers to whom it allows a period of credit before they have to make payments for their purchases. This period (usually expressed in days) represents the length of time that the company's money is being used by its customers to fund their purchases. Some companies, of course, may wish to use an extended period of credit to customers as a marketing tool by which to attract business away from their competitors.

Contrarily, by restricting the amount of time that customers use the company's money, the company can also reduce its own need for cash – obviously, since it has to fund a less extensive (and expensive) tail of business.

The ratio is calculated by the following expression:

(Debtors [or receivables]/turnover) × *365*

This will produce a value in days which represents the average amount of time that the company waits before it gets in money from sales. Extending the debt collection period may be a result of a number of different pressures as Chapter Eight will show.

Creditor days are shown in exactly the same way.

(Creditors [or payables]/turnover) × *365*

In this case what is being derived is the length of time that the company is able to use its suppliers' money before it has to pay them. (This may lead to consequential changes in other ratios – as was noted above in the example of supermarkets often having very low quick ratios). Companies in trouble often try to extend the length of time that they take to pay their suppliers and once they are under significant pressure, the length of creditor days often shrinks as suppliers try to limit their exposure to bad debts by allowing less and less credit. The continual gradual extension – or very rapid extension or contraction – of creditor days may be an indicator of trouble. But, as before, single-cause or single example reasons are often unsatisfactory in explaining company behaviour and may be misleading; Chapter Eight, again, will give some examples.

Stock turn can be taken as a proxy measure for a company's efficiency in generating sales. The faster that raw materials are turned into saleable stock from which the company can derive income, then (all other things being equal) the better will be the profit margin overall (not necessarily, though, on individual items).

Stock turn is calculated using the expression

Value of stock at year-end/turnover

This will give a number which indicates how much the stock changed during the year in terms of an approximate (and theoretical) value of how many times the company got through the stock it had on hand.

An apparently fast stock turn, though, can conceal a number of trends. This is because it is a composite of a number of factors – the movement in both volume and value of individual raw materials; the change in the holdings and value of semi-finished goods; sales of items made by the company – some large and some small; and, in some cases involving large projects, the effect of sales made over more than one year but with profit only fully recorded in the final year.

Very few large companies sell one product made from a combination of only two or three components, so the number that is derived from their balance sheets for the stock turn is the result of many, many individual movements all jumbled up into one value. Because of this the stock turn is most valuable when it is used in combination with values from previous years, to indicate trends and should not be regarded as a definitive indicator. (Other stock ratios that are income based will be dealt with in the next chapter.)

The final balance sheet ratio – the *net asset value* (NAV) – is of less interest in helping to predict future values about trading than in helping potential investors to determine the worth of the company they are looking at in comparison with other possible investments. It has greater meaning in this comparative fashion than it does in identifying any particular value.

The NAV is calculated by the following expression

[Total assets (current and non-current) plus shareholders equity (including share premium and reserves)] less [total liabilities (current and non-current)]/the number of shares in issue.]

It will be given as some value of pence per share.

A variant – the fully diluted NAV – takes into account the number of shares that will be in issue when all options and warrants, however derived, become eligible to share in profits. This fully diluted value will obviously be a smaller value – pence per share – than the undiluted value, since the number of shares used in the calculation will be greater.

As with all ratios, the best use is in comparison with a trend of previous years' values. Using the NAV can also reveal if a company is undervalued by the market – which sometimes does happen (for a variety of reasons) – when some companies (insurance businesses or investment trust for instance) are valued on their assets rather than simply on the growth of profitability. It can also be used in determining how attractive a company is in the event of a takeover bid, since very few companies would wish to see their own NAV diluted by the addition of a company with a lesser NAV – unless there were very cogent commercial reasons outweighing a simple calculation of value.

CHAPTER 6

Exploding and exploring the Income Statement

Individual items explained in greater detail

The major income statement ratios

    The gross margin

    The net margin

    Finance costs

    Operating ratios

INDIVIDUAL ITEMS EXPLAINED IN GREATER DETAIL

For most people the income statement – the profit and loss account – is probably what they first think of when they think of 'accounts'.

It is the dynamic bit of the report and accounts collection – and the bit that attracts attention in the press and on radio and TV and among share traders, since it shows the amount of money that the company has 'earned' during the period under consideration. This large figure, usually in millions of pounds for large quoted companies, is then converted into *earnings per share* – which then directly affects the share price through the multiple known as the *PE ratio*. Because of this there is usually a lot of movement in the share price just before and just after the release of the half-yearly or annual 'results' – the Income Statement for each six or twelve months – as shareholders and potential shareholders adjust their perceptions of what companies are worth.

But there are other, fundamental, ratios which are probably of greater continuing importance to the analysts available from the income statement.

Since the income statement is all about profits, most of these ratios are to do with *costs* and how they vary between years for the same company – and between companies, in both the same year and different years. This is because investors are usually looking for evidence that costs are being pushed down to their lowest possible levels (in order to provide the maximum levels of profit from any given turnover so as to release profit to them in the form of dividends).

Managers (most of them) will share this view but should – if they are sensible – realise that there is also a floor to the cost structure – what might be called the long-term sustainable level of costs (which might not be the lowest possible at any given time) – which will ensure the long-term viability of the company.

The problem for managers is that other companies are always finding ways of reducing *their* costs – through innovation, efficiency or even unfounded top-management *diktat* – and so every set of managers is constantly under the cosh to reduce costs as much as possible. Once costs have been reduced to this level (or sustainably close to it), no more profit can be squeezed out of that level of turnover without damaging the business.

If profit is going to be increased, then turnover has to expand (this could mean that selling prices are increased, of course). Assuming prices are not increased, the growth of turnover has to be achieved either organically or by acquisition. This means either expanding the company's market(s) by adding products, for instance – or by adding on the turnover of other companies to the base company (which then becomes the holding company for a developing group). Then the dance of reducing costs begins all over again.

THE MAJOR INCOME STATEMENT RATIOS

The easiest way to look at the ratios is to run down the IS statement, looking at each component in turn and identifying what the ratio for each can show about the company's finances. Emphatically, though, this is not a priority order for the ratios – some might be considered to be more valuable than others in determining company health or predicting future activity. Their value will be indicated as they are brought into focus.

The gross margin

The first ratio, gross margin, is an indication of the core ability of the company to turn income into basic profit.

Revenue less cost of sales = gross profit (or gross margin)

The gross margin is usually expressed as a percentage. So in the case of the Rotork 2013 accounts:

(Revenue)   *(CoS)*   *(gross profit)*

578440 − 304066 = 274374

or

gross profit equals 47% of sales (274374/578440).

All other costs have to come out of the gross profit so the higher it is the better. It is a fundamental indicator of the efficiency of the company and much management activity will be devoted to improving the gross margin. As such it is a very useful indicator of management capability – especially when used as a comparator with other companies in the same business.

It is necessary here to sound a caution about turnover and its comparison.

It is critically important when analysing accounts to read the small print that makes up the notes to the accounts – and especially so when considering turnover. Companies which make and sell a very great amount of very small items in a year – perhaps a confectionery company – will have a definition of what turnover is that may be quite different from, say, a large bridge builder whose individual products may take a couple of years to complete. The turnover of these two will be calculated quite differently from each other.

This may appear to be capricious. How can a concept such as turnover be different in one case from another? The clue to unravelling this is in thinking what turnover is. It is the value of goods *sold during the period under review*. And this has to accord with the concept that guides all accounting – that there should be a 'true and fair view' of the state of the company's finances presented in the audited accounts

A sweet manufacturer may sell millions of peppermints in a year, but a bridge manufacturer may only 'sell' half a bridge in the same period. Such a definition is then patently absurd since no one buys half a bridge; so the accounting definitions in each case have to take into account the time it takes to complete a sale, if they are going to mean anything at all. If that then were to be taken as 'the period under review' there would be no consistency in the timing of accounts – there would be huge disparities between companies' reporting periods, in fact. The sweet-maker might be content with a twelve-month period while the bridge-maker mighty want a period that varied between, say, eighteen and thirty months.

Consequently, accountants – who may be the least capricious profession on earth (only less capricious than actuaries, who considered a career in accounting to be too exciting for them) – have given themselves some conceptual leeway, to better accord with reality, by allowing companies to measure turnover (and take profits on that turnover) in slightly different ways. The notes to the accounts should make clear the exact nature of the way that turnover is calculated and profit is taken – hence their critical importance.

Another feature of gross margin is that some companies with huge (volume) turnovers of (usually) fast-moving individual items, can afford to have very modest gross margins – supermarkets typically have gross margins at or even less than 5%. If they sell enough product often enough even at a very low individual margin, there will still be a welter of cash into the business to pay all the other costs.

So gross margin can also be an indication of the *sort* of business that is under examination. If a group has a gross margin markedly different from nominally similar groups, then it may not be simply that the management is better or worse than those being compared: it could be that there are different types of business in the group whose effects may be to sweeten or depress the composite margin.

Most companies have a composite gross margin – formed of some high margin products and some lower ones. The gross margin calculated from the accounts won't be an absolute value but will be a jumble of different individual margins. This, once again, emphasises the importance of using all ratios in a comparative fashion to compare an individual company's progress over time or to evaluate one company against another.

Back to examining individual costs. The costs of sales that the company bears are often referred to as *prime costs* by economists or *direct costs* by accountants. All the other costs that the company faces are therefore *indirect costs*.

These indirect costs can still form a hefty burden on gross profits. There are a variety of ways of determining the apportionment of costs between distribution and administration costs. For the analyst's purposes it doesn't matter what they are as long as they are consistent (and herein lies a way of making mischief as Chapter Eleven will show). So, once again, looking at these indirect costs is best done over a period of time and in comparison with other businesses.

The net margin

In contrast to the gross margin, the net margin is the amount of profit that the company generates after *all* costs have been taken into account. Arithmetically, it is the pre-tax profit divided by the turnover.

It is also used as a measure of company efficiency but is affected by all the intermediate costs (dealt with below) faced by the company and so can be rather a blunt instrument in analytical terms. Its use comes when comparing two companies in the same area of business with similar gross margins but different net margins, where it alerts the analyst to a difference in the way that the companies are run and the costs bases that they face.

But there is a slight wrinkle here. As well as comparing these two components individually over time (vertically) and with other similar businesses (horizontally), by checking on them as a *proportion of total costs* it becomes possible to see if the costs of running the business itself are getting more burdensome.

All large businesses are nothing more than profit-seeking bureaucracies in conceptual terms. There is a prevalence among all bureaucracies to replicate themselves if at all possible in order to expand their span of power (this is in fact one of the defining characteristics of a bureaucracy). The budgetary mechanism, often more strictly applied in profit-seeking businesses than the public sector (which lacks the measure of profit against which to judge value) is one of the leashes by which they are controlled. But in any organisation there may still be a creeping tendency for administrative costs to increase over time.

FINANCE COSTS

The next structural element of the income statement is that which relates to *finance costs*. The important part of this is as a check on the debt in the balance sheet. A low level of debt should mean that there is a modest finance charge. If the company has a small level of debt at the end of the year but a much larger interest charge than would be expected then obviously something needs to be explained.

The primary likelihood is that there is a pronounced difference in debt during the year than is represented by the year-end debt value. (If the debt at the end of the year is much lower than at the start then this would also be an explanation). Typically companies choose their year-end to flatter their balance sheets, choosing the months that show the lowest levels of debt and stocks and the highest levels of cash. So it may well be that the interest charge looks 'wrong' and needs to be put in the context of the use of debt through the year. Reconciling the Income statement with the Sources and Uses statement and with the balance sheet values helps this.

There are also some ratios which cross boundaries between the income statement and the balance sheet but which are known as *operating ratios* because they give a clue to the efficiency of the way that the company is being run.

THE OPERATING RATIOS

There are three major operating ratios:

the *gross profit margin* – dealt with above

the *return on capital employed (ROCE)*; and

sales to capital employed

The return on capital employed is a traditional measure of profitability, which gives interesting insights into the efficiency of the company.

First it is a measure of the vulnerability of profits to a downturn in activity. In an economic recession, ROCE can easily be extinguished – in which case the shareholders would be better off with their money in the bank.

Second, if the ROCE is lower than the cost of borrowing then any form of increased borrowing (in an effort to boost earnings) will wipe out the earnings per share.

Third, it acts as a guide for the value of potential acquisitions – if the potential combined ROCE is low then despite other attractions, the acquisition is probably not sensible.

Last, the reverse of the last point, is that if a part of the group has an ROCE persistently lower than the rest of the group, it should be a disposal candidate.

ROCE is calculated using the following expression:

Trading profit / [share capital + reserves + all borrowings + minority interests + provisions] less associated company interests less investments

(Minority interests are the shareholdings that the group may hold in companies which are below the threshold to be counted as associated companies – in other words below 25% of the equity of these companies).

It should be apparent that any revaluation of the company's assets will have the effect of *increasing* the capital employed and therefore *reducing* the ROCE. This is one of the reasons which explains – apart from the fact that the directors have the option of doing so – why so much company property is held at the lesser of purchase price and market value.

Sales against capital employed is a measure of sales efficiency and is expressed as a multiple. Its use is limited, apart from internal usage by managers who may be able to ascribe accurate values. For the outsider, apart from a vertical analysis of one company there is so much divergence between companies in terms of the constitution of the numbers that form the ratio that a comparative value is pretty much unreliable as a guide to a company's performance.

A small digression – EBITDA

If you read the financial commentaries you may occasionally come across a measure of a company's performance using the acronym *EBITDA.*

This stands for

earnings before interest, tax, depreciation and amortisation.

It purports to show what is called 'free cash flow earnings' and is supposed to show the effect of trading purified from financing decisions.

It is, actually, a useless measure since it postulates an entirely artificial world where depreciation does not exist and where the normal rules of prudent accounting do not apply. For the analyst, it is La-La Land accounting – the financial equivalent of someone sticking their fingers in their ears and humming loudly if they don't want to hear what is being said. It's like saying, 'Well everything would have looked like this, if this . . . and this . . . and this . . . and this, hadn't happened'.

That having been said, companies sometimes use it as a measure in a specialised way when they wish to show a very particular pattern of activity for internal purposes.

Now that we have despatched that particular piece of frippery, you can ignore it and forget it. Analysts who use it probably don't know what they are talking about.

CHAPTER 7

Exploding and exploring the Sources and Uses Statement

The dictates of the structure

A practical structure

How the S&U illuminates the accounts

The limitations of the S&U

The S&U and 'red flags'

And almost a misuse . . . free flow cash

There are no formal ratios to examine in this section – because the sources and uses is a synthetic structure, derived from the information in the income statement and the balance sheet, all the ratio work has been done in those sections.

That does not mean that there is no need to compare and contrast information in the same way that information from the other parts of the accounts has been subjected to analysis. Contrasting the way that cash flows change year on year is an extremely sensitive indicator of developing or deteriorating value (and potential problems). The sources and uses of cash also are significant in forecasting profits into the future, since changes in working capital usage, as turnover expands or contracts, help predict finance charges and turnover margins (gross to some extent but net particularly).

What is particularly important to recognise is that, while setbacks in profits can be weathered by most companies if they are reasonably mature, continuing deteriorations in the cash position of a company signify either an imminent need to re-finance – or something even more painful. Companies that run out of cash find life very hard – they are at the mercy of their creditors and shareholders are often then forced to add to the cash resources of the company at a time of weakness. 'Turnover is vanity – cash is sanity'!

THE DICTATES OF THE STRUCTURE

There is a fixed format to the sources and uses of funds because of the potentially ambiguous nature of some of the components. This is governed by an *international financial reporting standard* – Financial Reporting Standard No. 1 (which obviously indicates how important the accounting authorities believe the issue to be).

The FRS 1 rules require the flows to be shown in the following order:

1. operating activities

2. returns on investments

3. taxation

4. capital expenditure and investments

5. costs/proceeds of acquisitions and disposals

6. equity dividends

7. liquid resources management

8. financing

Despite the apparent simplicity and logic of the FRS format, it doesn't really accord with practical pressures. By far the most volatile part of the sources and uses is the amount of money that has to be devoted to working capital – the sum of stock; debtors and creditors. This is not beyond the power of the managers to control but is a very powerful engine for producing fundamental alterations in the company's financial structure. Not all of these will be working in the direction that the managers want the company to go.

A PRACTICAL STRUCTURE

A simpler, practical explanation of the usual order, which does explain some of the pressures goes like this:

1. The starting point for the Sources and Uses is the pre-tax profits (as reported) with depreciation added back (because depreciation, although charged, carries no movement of cash).

2. The next component is additional (positive or negative) funds from other (normal) activities – the proceeds of disposals (which can be negative if a loss is recorded on disposals) returns on investments and the income from a cash pile, if the company has one.

3. Then comes 'No-choice' expenditure – tax and debt and debt-servicing payments.

4. After that there is 'Some choice' expenditure – the level of dividends. Dividends are usually expected by shareholders to rise gradually, if possible.

The result of those sums is:

5. The amount of money that the company finds devoted to stock increases (or if stock holdings are decreasing this can be used to supplement income as a negative expenditure). This can be sometimes offset (or increased) by changes in debtors and creditors, which can move both in the same direction or in opposite directions as far as cash is concerned.

6. Only after that comes the money that the board can then allocate to capital expenditure and growing the business.

This doesn't follow the formal priority of the FRS but it does show that the Sources and Uses represents the outcome of a balancing act for the company. It shows the outcome of the policies chosen in playing off all the competing pressures on the company's finances, all of which are set against the background of the trading conditions faced by the company.

HOW THE S&U ILLUMINATES THE ACCOUNTS

Obviously, what it can also show is that the room to manoeuvre is sometimes heavily constrained. The pressures from some of the components will be greater than others. The S&U can show us how much pressure some of these components are having – regardless of what managers would like to do.

For instance – if the stock levels are increasing very fast year on year, such that the company has to increase borrowing because the sum of pre-tax profits and disposals is not adequate to provide the cash, then it is probable that the company is facing some very difficult trading conditions. There are very few circumstances where managers will borrow to finance additional stock holdings: building strategic stocks might be one; or anticipating a price rise might be another – but these pressures would have to be pretty hefty to warrant the additional costs of finance on these stocks.

The intention of FRS1 is to make the flows as clear as possible. The FRS requires a statement by the company reconciling net debt with the movement of cash.

But there are some problems which need to be disclosed separately – for instance, some international companies may have problems in remitting cash generated in one jurisdiction into their home territory.

Cash which is locked in one jurisdiction (either because of market reasons like lack of practical convertibility or because of political regulations prohibiting removal) cannot be used to fund expenditure elsewhere. So this information has to be shown separately in the notes to the accounts if it applies (yet another in the long list of reasons for a detailed scrutiny of the notes *before* any other work is done on the individual components of the accounts!).

Similarly, not all the proceeds from 'the share of profits from associated companies' will produce cash. Sometimes timing payments will affect this. Sometimes the profits may not be the same as dividends received. Companies are also required to show where this is the case.

THE LIMITATIONS OF THE S&U

The S&U is a critical component of any forecasting process looking to be more than guesswork about turnover. But it does have limitations and these need to be recognised.

As with all the other parts of the accounts, the S&U is a historical document. It shows what happened but it does not show very much about *why* it happened, although some circumstantial inferences can be drawn.

But more usually than not there can be multiple explanations for any one financial 'event' as displayed in the S&U – and the outside analyst will have no way (usually) of determining which is one is the possessor of the superior likelihood. (Sometimes, of course, the narrative part of the report will describe pretty clearly why one thing happened.)

To expand the example given above about stock increases, there are at least four explanations beyond the two already indicated (strategic stock-building or anticipated price increases). The stock position could also have increased because the management were anticipating a shortage of a critical component or raw material; because stocks were being built up prior to the launch of a new product; because products hadn't sold as well as anticipated; or because stock control had broken down. Even that list is not exhaustive.

A similar exercise for a change in receivables (debtors) might be because payments have slowed (debtors rarely pay earlier than they have to); or because there has been a change in credit policy; or because the accounts department has got into trouble; or simply because turnover has increased and the credit terms have remained the same. Again, that's far from being an exhaustive list.

Occasionally companies appear to have large amounts of debt and large amounts of cash at the same time. An outsider might think this is an indication of poor cash management. It is more likely an indication of different reasons for keeping both cash and debt which could be caused by any one of the following (or a combination of them):

1. timing differences in expenditure;

2. differences in exchange rates between countries;

3. differences in interest rates between countries;

4. remittance considerations;

5. tax planning considerations;

6. debt maturity considerations

and so and so on . . .

THE S&U AND 'RED FLAGS'

The S&U will give a flag for further investigation but it will not necessarily – not normally – provide a conclusive reason for something it shows. For that it is often necessary to look at the narrative part of the accounts, which is considered in the next chapter, or to combine one or two pieces of information together from the S&U (and/or the balance sheet and/or the income statement) and make a heroic guess (which, if it turns out to be correct, transmutes into a reasoned deduction).

This is where a flair for being able to piece disparate fragments of information benefits the analyst. Looking for corroborative information comes with practice but a good start can often be made by thinking about the fundamental characteristics of a business – its seasonality; the international spread of its operations; does it have high volume turnover or high value turnover?

The historical nature of the S&U can also be put to good use in supplying information that is not easily found elsewhere. For instance, in comparison to the Income Statement, which shows the tax anticipated to be charged for the year, the S&U shows the tax *actually paid* – which gives something of a clue to the profitability of the business for the year previous to that being reported on.

Accounting for tax
Although the last statement above is basically correct, great care must be exercised, as tax is not an easy subject to deal with accurately at this introductory level.

A corporation tax payment is another instance of a composite number formed of lots of different components involving tax reliefs, tax rates and the potential tax burden spread across different countries. Again, this information is much more useful when viewed in aggregated trends than when taken in isolation.

AND ALMOST A MISUSE . . . FREE CASH FLOW

The final complicating aspect of the uses to which the S&U can be put, is that it can also be used to show a value (for so-called *free cash flow*) for which there is not a conclusive definition, or for which companies sometimes supply their own definitions.

Free cash flow is supposedly a measure of the cash-generative ability of the company in normal circumstances (and is usually quoted on a per share basis). The practical version of the priorities for the S&U listed at the start of the chapter illustrated the limited room for manoeuvre that managers usually have in discretionary use of the cash generated by the company. A welter of money from sources is often matched by a tidal wave of outflow into uses that are pretty much pre-determined.

Accounting theorists don't care very much about this since the uses to which the sources are put are not of great theoretical interest in themselves. But the concept may be valuable to companies in trying to prove a point to their own shareholders or in comparing their own business and that of a competitor – or particularly in examining a potential acquisition. No company wants to go through the ordeal of buying another only to find that what it has bought then sucks up cash like a one-armed bandit.

The irrelevance and absurdities of EBITDA, which purports to show free cash flow, has already been dealt with (on page 62) so that need not be revisited. But, regardless of that criticism, the concept of 'free cash flow' is occasionally used by companies for their own purposes – when considering the cash-flow effects of an acquisition, for instance.

What is incontestable is that it is of, at best, negligible limited use as a predictive tool. In the case of one company acquiring another (where it might be used) the definition of the terms is all important. There is often a wide divergence in definitions of the concept between companies (because the concept is more than a bit shaky for all but acquisition studies). In such circumstances, one of two stances can be adopted by the analyst, if there seems to be a pressing need to explain or understand the EBITDA examples given by companies.

Either, a consistent definition is applied by the analyst, regardless of what the company under examination uses, or the notes to the accounts are scrutinised and the definition preferred by the company is applied.

Occasionally financial commentaries carry details of the results EBITDA calculations made by stock-broking analysts when one company announces an intention to bid for another. These reports usually indicate that the journalist had no idea of what the terms means and was just slavishly copying notes of a conversation with a broker – and that the broker was trying to baffle with jargon and didn't have much idea either of the significant limitations of the concept.

In most cases it is extremely difficult to see what benefit an EBITDA calculation could have for an outside observer since it doesn't add much to understanding. First, if it is going to be done, the calculations can be better performed with inside knowledge of the sort that would come with a much fuller understanding of the companies involved than can usually be gained from outside. Second, for an observer to merely repeat the calculations performed by company insiders is a pointless activity anyway.

However, since the concept is sometimes used, it would be wise to know what the terms means and so, for illustrative purposes only, one definition of free cash flow – the one that probably has the most resilience to manipulation and least possibility of misinterpretation – is given below.

Free cash flow per share = [cash flow from operations (after finance costs) + return on investments – tax paid] / weighted average of ordinary shares in issue in the period.

The moral of this is that free cash flow – supposedly a measure of the cash-generating ability of any given business – is a concept which has to be validated for each and every company by reference to the definitions that the company gives in its own notes. Yet another addition to the list of reasons why the analyst should read the notes to the Accounts first!

CHAPTER 8

The narrative report – and the notes to the accounts

Size – shape and volume

Structure and form

Purpose

Current information requirements

Other crucial information

Up to this point several references have already been made about the importance of reading the notes to the accounts.

Given that all the major numerical parts of the accounts have now been examined and explored in some detail, it is now appropriate to look at the narrative part of the accounts – the report (more properly called the directors' report) – and the notes that supplement the numerical information.

SIZE – SHAPE AND VOLUME

The size of the report section has expanded inexorably year after year for all companies on the London Stock Exchange as the (now obligatory) requirements of the UK Governance Code have expanded. Whether this expansion has been valuable is moot. Volume does not always equate to value.

In many cases, the volume of the information provided in the report serves to obscure information by being both too extensive and too shallow at the same time. The sort of company information that might be of use is further camouflaged by the ludicrous 'comply or explain' principle that has ruled corporate governance thinking for the past thirty years – companies that don't want to comply with the rules don't have to if they say why they think they shouldn't. Since these explanations are never good enough – merely couched as variants of 'the directors don't think it necessary '—the whole exercise is reduced to a very low common denominator.

Be all that as it may, what can the report section tell the analyst about the company's most recent year?

The simple answer is that every page will tell the analyst something of importance. Every company will be different – so generalisations will have to do for the most part – but using the Rotork accounts as a guide, once more, some of the information that can be gleaned from a careful reading of the notes will become apparent.

THE STRUCTURE AND FORM

All accounts are divided into roughly the same sections:

1. the strategic report

2. the report of the directors

3. the 'governance' report

4. the financial statements

5. simple information about the company (group) such as

   - a financial calendar (perhaps)
   - a ten-year financial history (perhaps)
   - a list of locations and addresses
   - names of advisers and so on.

Each of these sections has a set of sub-sections containing information that the Stock Exchange requires companies to disclose.

The Strategic Report

● Summary of the year – sometimes called 'highlights'

● Geographical locations of the group's operations

● An overview of the company's marketplace(s)

● A description of the company's strategy

● The chairman's statement

● A review by the chief executive (some companies also have a finance director's review)

● A review of the business broken down into business or product segments

● A financial review – usually where the FD's report is found

● Key Performance Indicators – compared with last year's at least

● Risk review – this section is highly variable in length between different companies

● 'Corporate Social Responsibility'

Summary of the year

This is usually in tabular format and will show the revenue; the operating profit; the pre-tax profit and the earnings per share for the current year (that is, the one being reported on) – all compared with the previous year.

Any additional information is at the discretion of the company.

All the information in this section will have been verified by the auditors (as will every piece of information in the report – written or computed).

Geographical locations

This section – which is often shown cartographically – is also supposed to include details of the size of operations (perhaps by employee numbers as well as turnover).

Marketplace overview

Breaking the company's products down into their major groupings, this section is also supposed to indicate what it is that influences markets – positively and negatively. It will show market share by type of product – as far as the company can determine it; some further details about product differentiation and probably also some indication of what the company sees as the major opportunities for growth.

Business Model

This section is the part of the report that companies use to show what they believe to be the strategic characteristics that mark them out from the competition. It may well explain why a certain acquisition has been made and what the company believes to be the consequential strengths of the combined grouping.

The strategic priorities the company identifies should then be used as a framework to show how it is developing its strategy by indicating the progress against Key Indicators which it will have identified in the last set of accounts and the objectives it will set itself for the coming year.

PURPOSE

The chairman's statement

This is the historical centre of the accounts since, by law, all companies are required to provide a statement from the directors to the shareholders explaining the prospects for the company in the coming year and have been required to do so for many years – virtually since the inception of the limited liability company.

It used to be the case that this section was very brief, told shareholders nothing and – almost as important – revealed nothing to the competition.

The legal format of the report and accounts

The modern structure of the statutory accounts is quite recent. Not until 1948 were companies required to produce accounts in the form from which the modern accounts are derived. And in the 1920s it was common for companies to produce accounts which contained secret provisions – disguised by the firm's accountants and the concealment approved by the auditors – from which to pay whatever dividends the directors thought fit (or not).

CURRENT INFORMATION REQUIREMENTS

The Stock Exchange now requires a much more fulsome narrative which often gives a great deal of additional detail about the company's activities. This now usually takes the form of two or three separate statements – one from the chairman dealing with an overview and board matters; one from the chief executive dealing with operational matters; and one from the finance director, dealing with financial and treasury matters.

In the case of the chairman's statement, since much of the factual information will have been covered in the preceding sections, it is necessary to look for more subtle phrasings rather than mere bald statements of fact. The chairman's statement often seems like the mortar in a brick wall helping to tie in statements from other sections to make a coherent whole.

The chief executive's statement

This is often where the real nuggets of information are found – details of margins for subsidiary companies that can be deduced from turnover and profit figures, for instance; or the detail of local markets or product offerings that help the derivation of further information about profitability on product lines; information about anticipated trading conditions that can then be fitted into a disaggregated forecast of profits.

This part of the report is supposed to deal both with 'normal' information and exceptional developments. It can give very valuable information on which to base speculative but reasoned estimates of turnover and profitability.

For instance, information about headcount in a subsidiary – often contained in the detail of this section – can be used to help estimate rates of growth of turnover, or the likely temporary dip in profitability that this may bring if the increase is forced (to rectify a problem in sales flow, maybe).

Since labour costs are usually the major part of a company's costs, increases in headcount are usually undertaken only if margin per worker can be maintained – or sales levels increased (more than proportionately) at the expense of some modest amount of margin per employee. So, as an example, a sudden increase in headcount by twenty-five could presage a big increase in profits from one subsidiary – and this might be reported on as being a significant event which will give a clue to trends.

Some companies take this obligation to explain very seriously and provide even more disaggregated information by division or product area, as does Rotork. These individual reports may provide subtle information about the progress of key contracts that is not easily picked up from other sources. Or it may, for instance, indicate that a very valuable long-term contract has been won which will underpin profitability for a specific division.

The financial review

The section, completed by the finance director, will give the analyst additional 'nuts-and-bolts' information about matters like borrowing, currency hedging and acquisition details. It will probably also reveal some of the anticipations of the managers' about key ratios like ROCE and working capital in the coming year.

The financial review will help with fine-tuning the non-operational aspects of producing reasonably accurate forecasts properly underpinned with supporting information.

Key Performance Indicators

This is the only remaining section of use to the analyst in forecasting information.

It will give details of how close the company is to making its own targets or, if there is some distance yet to go, how it intends to achieve those targets. Sometimes these tables may provide further information by synthesis – by coupling something in the KPI tables with a piece of information from one of the other reports.

Corporate Governance and remaining information

The remaining information in the report is determined by the obligations of the UK Stock Exchange Listing agreement and deals with the corporate governance of the company and how well it conforms to best practice.

This section takes up increasing amounts of space and is of little real value in predictive terms. It does provide a contextual benefit to the potential investor though, since companies which are poorly governed (that is, without observation of the obligations of 'good' corporate governance) are usually avoided by professional investors (who often have internal corporate obligations placed on them to invest in 'respectable' companies). This may mean that such companies are relatively shunned in terms of market activity – perhaps the prospects for profit growth are not fully reflected in their share prices because investors have reservations about the managerial structure or nepotism or succession planning, for instance.

There must now also be a section detailing specifically the remuneration of the directors. This section was originally intended to be *substantive* – it was to have been available for shareholders to vote on and, most importantly, that the vote was intended to have weight. If the vote went against the company, then the directors' plans for paying themselves would have to be reconsidered.

After lobbying, this was watered down so that although shareholders vote on the report, the outcome of the vote is merely 'noted' by the company who are supposed to take the vote into consideration the next time they fix their pay.

Such votes are always accompanied by statements from the chairmen of the remuneration committees that they will do exactly that – but the numbers of times it happens is a small proportion of the number of times that there are adverse votes.

There will also be quite a lot of information about the company's social responsibilities. This, again, is of very little value to the process of understanding the company's financial dynamics. (To be only mildly cynical such activity, with very, very few exceptions, serves little practical purpose other than to burnish the company's self-image and the pointless purpose of massaging egos in the boardroom).

Bribery

As a consequence of the Bribery Act of 2010, all UK companies must now carry a reference to their policy in respect of bribery and corruption. This *must* be on the company's website but some also carry it through to the report and accounts. Because of the statutory obligation, an inclusion here must not be taken as an indication of anything being wrong or any form of weakness in the company's finances.

Despite numerous instances of companies being caught out in misbehaviour – some even since the passage of the Bribery Act – company directors are obliged under the terms of the 2010 Act to show by means of a statement on the company website and in its accounts that they regard bribery and corruption as A Bad Thing. On the evidence of some companies' past performance, though, a more truthful account would say that while they do not condone the practice, they are happy to use bribery as method of winning international contracts if circumstances require and the rewards justify it. That would at least be honest!

The report of the directors

This section, which used to be core of the report for many years as one of the few parts required by law, has now been relegated to almost insignificance and is merely a matter of record for otherwise fairly trivial details.

Long-term record

The pages just prior to the inside back cover are often used by companies to give details of their long-term financial record and details of when shares go 'ex-dividend'; when dividends are paid; when company meetings are due and when financial announcements will be made.

The value of these pages is often overlooked. The information they provide is very useful.

The long-term record – which usually includes not just information about turnover; pre-tax profit; and dividends but is often a summary of the Income Statement – is of considerable importance in displaying trends which may not be apparent from a two- or three-year run which can be obtained from a couple of sets of accounts. Getting that information from other sources can often be time-consuming and tedious, although of course, there is nothing to explain the detail of particular numbers and the context has to be conjectured if the analyst is not familiar with the company's history.

The timings of shares going 'ex-div' and the dates of announcements are also of crucial importance in explaining short-term price movements.

Companies issue dividends on the basis of possession of shares at a certain date. Shareholders whose names are on the register of shareholders at a certain date (the 'record date') are entitled to receive the dividend – *even though they may no longer possess the shares at the time the dividend is paid* (because of settlement timings – the difference between buying or selling a share and actually paying for it or receiving the money for it).

Obviously a share in company A with the right to receive a dividend is – all other things being equal – of more value than the same share in company A which has no such rights. So the day after the shares go 'ex-div' it is usual to see the share price dip slightly as buyers take into account the fact that a dividend right is no longer attached. Similarly in the few days *before* a share goes ex-div, there might be some upward movement in the price as investors who want income buy the shares to get the right to the dividend.

Selling shares with and without dividends

Why should anyone wish to sell shares while they have the dividend right attached?

There are some professional investors who are concerned only with the growth of capital in their funds and these may well be sellers of shares just before the ex-div date as they anticipate a fall in value following the ex-div point which will disturb their growth record.

Dates of announcements of financial results

Are also valuable for the same reason – share prices often become volatile around the date of release of financial information and the investor should be aware of these in order to minimise losses or maximise gains.

Company websites

In almost every case, all this information will now be on the company's website to a greater or lesser degree, since the law now requires listed companies to run appropriate websites for the benefit of shareholders – and of course the website has the benefit of being continually updated (and also of carrying lots of historical detail). Because of its dynamic nature, the website has become of crucial importance to the analyst in ensuring that the information being worked with is up-to-date.

Information about other types of company interaction with the City – analysts meetings; presentations to investors and so on – are also often posted on the section of the website devoted to investors' interests. (Some companies maintain separate websites for this – insurance and other financial companies keep their customers' and investors' websites separate for obvious reasons.)

Companies often use the website to make announcements of contracts won or large orders placed or other trading information. All this information has to go simultaneously for release through the Stock Exchange so it is (in theory) available to everyone. But keeping track of all this information through the press, radio and TV or the Stock Exchange's own website is a difficult and time-consuming task.

As far as the analyst is concerned, trying to see inside the workings of a group of companies from the outside, small pieces of information about trading, contracts or other matters that the company discloses and then records in one place are very helpful in drawing up an accurate picture of the company. The value of the website in drawing together, and keeping together, all this information is considerable.

PART THREE

APPLYING

CHAPTER 9

The Income Statement – predicting changes in profits

Starting at the top

Assumptions and iteration

'Equivalent halves'

The basic technique of forecasting

Using information from other accounts sections

Iteration – again!

Chapter Nine begins the sequence of three chapters which look at applying the information that has been gleaned from analysing the report and accounts to produce forecasts of how companies' finances might look for the purposes of investment evaluation.

The order adopted until now has been to look at the balance sheet, then the income statement and then the sources and uses, showing how each is linked together by pieces of information that bridge them all.

This approach will now be changed to reflect the priority that stock market investors attach to earnings per share as the determinant of share prices (and also the easiest and most practical way of making profit forecasts). Earnings are determined principally by profits – so the income statement is the place to start the forecasting exercise (although some information from the balance sheet and the S&U will be used to supplement the sequence of the process).

The sequence of forecasting is very much what might be expected – start at the top with forecasting turnover and then work down through all the categories of cost to arrive at a pre-tax earnings figure. The resulting figure is then reduced by a 'normal' or 'standard' tax charge and divided by the number of shares in issue to give earnings per share (or the average number of shares during the period to give *diluted earnings*; or even the maximum that could be considered to be in issue to give *fully diluted earnings*). That then can be used to show whether the company is expensive, cheap or fairly priced against its own record or against its comparators or against different and alternative investments.

However – it is a little bit more complicated than that. If any attempt is to be made at producing a forecast which has a reasonable grounding in reality, it has to be based on a reasoned set of assumptions.

STARTING AT THE TOP

The turnover of a group is the combination of all the component parts of the group. While making a simple percentage addition might just be right – with a great deal of luck – it is unlikely to produce accurate results on a repeatable basis, because of this mix of trends, values and dynamics.

What has to be stated here very emphatically is that a forecast is not going to be 'right' in anything but the total amount if it is anywhere near the figure that the group eventually reports.

There is not a human being alive – or dead or yet to be born come to that matter – who can forecast any financial dynamic with accuracy for a period of greater than six months and still less on a repeatable basis, other than through pure luck.

Most forecasts that happen to coincide with the number actually reported are nothing more than lucky coincidences of digits. When broken down into components, the best that can be hoped for is that the trends of individual components all point in the correct direction.

It is this trend movement that a sensible analyst strives to predict – not a spurious accuracy of a composite value for a group of numbers that in reality is just the outcome of chance.

ASSUMPTIONS AND ITERATION

The central basis of sensible forecasting is to build up a composite based on information that tries to reflect the company/group's activity in its various markets. For instance, in looking at the information in the report that deals with market size, strategy and individual operational reports it may have been possible to 'cross-pollinate' information. It may be obvious from the narrative in the divisional directors' reports or from the statistics given that the turnover from one division is down to activity in just one major territory or one major product.

Careful evaluation of the information given will help to reveal quite a lot about the way that turnover for the group is made up.

One formal way of doing this is to compile a matrix of information with member companies of the group listed along one axis and territories along the other. (An alternative would be to produce a matrix with products along one axis and territories along the other axis – whatever fits the available information best).

An example of what such a (skeleton) matrix might look like is shown below:

Forecasting matrix for a housebuilder

	H1	H2	FYa	H1	H2	FYb	H1	H2	FYc
Turnover									
Unit sales									
Average price									
% chge									

Figure 6: A forecasting matrix

Putting the known information into the boxes allows a picture to be built up of roughly where turnover comes from – half year by half year (H1 and H2) and then for the full year (FY). There will inevitably be gaps and some judicious estimates (read: reasoned guesses) will have to be made. But the object should be clear – to try to break down the overall turnover figure for the last couple of half-year reports into smaller disaggregated totals that can then be forecasted with slightly more justification.

Slipped into that last sentence is another key concept. Companies report their financial results on a six-monthly basis in the UK. The first half numbers are followed some time later by the total for the full year. By deducting the half year from the full year results (for the same financial year) it is possible to build up a picture of the way that turnover was built up over the year, showing first half, second half and then full year.

Very obviously, the full year results (FY) are the total of the two half years (H1 and H2). If you know both the first half-year (H1) figures and the full year results then by elimination you also know the second half numbers too. To express that statement slightly differently,

$$FY-H1=H2$$

The information revealed by this simple parsing of the financial results can be a powerful aid to forecasting, since it can be manipulated arithmetically to reveal trends of fundamental importance in understanding how a company wins its profits.

'EQUIVALENT HALVES'

Some companies have very skewed half years, where one six-month period consistently shows a larger turnover than the other. Some companies exhibit consistent growth consecutive half-on-half. Some companies (only a few) have no real relationship between the halves (not surprisingly these are the most difficult to forecast and tend to be undervalued in consequence because of persistent uncertainty and the likelihood of shocks).

By knowing which of these categories the company being analysed falls into (which can be deduced from examining a run of half years and calculating the percentage increases half-on-half or half-by-half) some of the pure guesswork about the tendency of the trend can be reduced.

In addition to all this, company managers know that investors value – above all else – an absence of shocks in their investments. Consistent returns are desirable and consistently and gently growing returns are more desirable. Managers take, quite legitimately, what leeway they are offered by the accounting rules to try to smooth their half-yearly results so as not to produce shocks.

An analyst who ignores this to produce a half-year results pattern greatly at variance with the past pattern will be either foolhardy, very sure of his or her forecasting ability – or *extremely* well informed by the sort of tip that is now probably outlawed by market regulations.

Insider trading

Thirty years ago, information was regularly imparted to analysts by company finance directors that would now get both of them into jail. Insider trading then was a very limited concept – far narrower than the rules now allow – and was made a criminal activity in 1980.

Insider trading is a complex area. The rules appear to be simple but the latitude for interpretation (and consequently for misbehaviour) is considerable.

Essentially the position is this:

A person is an *insider* if they have information not generally available to the market on which it could reasonably assumed that there would be a movement in the share price if it were to be acted upon.

Insider dealing takes place when this information is used.

The penalties for those convicted of insider dealing can be very severe – fines; imprisonment; confiscation of the presumed proceeds of the deals.

Sometimes the report and accounts give so much information about the basis of the company's turnover that it is reasonably easy to construct a forecasting model for turnover. This is often the case with house-building companies, which are often among the easiest to analyse because of the relative simplicity of their product and the close tie-in they have (usually) with the economic cycle.

As an exercise in seeing what information companies provide and how to make use of it, go to the website for Barratt Developments plc and use the very extensive information there – all helpfully provided by the company itself – to begin to complete a forecasting matrix. The information can all be found at www.barrattdevelopments.co.uk.

Click on the sub-head along the top which is entitled 'Investors' and then go to the section headed 'Reports, Results and Presentations' in the drop-down menu. Using the information in the half-year accounts and the full-year report for the most recent year *for which all the information is available* (which will obviously change from time to time), it is easy to see how many completions and sales Barratt reported in the first half of any given year, then interpolate the value for the second half by taking the full-year total and deducting the half-year from it. This information can go into the forecasting matrix shown above.

Barratt very helpfully provides an average selling price (ASP) for all its properties, broken down by sector. This is derived by dividing the aggregate turnover for the sector – private, affordable and joint venture – by the number of houses sold to give an average price per sale in the period. Like all averages it will conceal a great deal (in this case of variance in prices between locations) but it is a very useful starting point for forecasting.

Barratt even goes so far as to show the percentage changes that it managed to achieve (usually upwards) in the margin that it derived from these sales by each half-year. This may well – probably will – show a nice progression half-on-half.

All this information can then be incorporated into a projection for the number of houses that the company is likely to complete in the forecast period (again all worked on a half-on-half basis) and taking a realistic position on the margins, will produce a turnover figure. After this projection has been made, the individual halves and the full-year should be scrutinised very critically to see if they make sense – and if there is a nice, smooth transition between the individual halves. The change between the current year and the projected year should not normally (unless there are specific and good reasons) be too extreme.

The rate of change year-on-year serves as a check on the forecasting assumptions. If the increase looks about right then it is fair to proceed with the argument and consequent projections in the current form. If not, the underlying suppositions have to be reviewed and revised until the final forecast does look broadly consistent with the evidence of the actual price per sale and the numbers of houses sold.

At some point in both the reports for both the half year and the full year (which will be included in the PDF versions on the website), the company gives an indication of trading conditions currently being experienced. It is obliged to do this by existing company law.

If the first half is being forecast, using that information against the equivalent half figures from the previous year (*always* use equivalent comparatives unless the company's phrasing makes it clear that it is commenting on half-by-half consecutively), the analyst can make a stab at forecasting the next period – always remembering that normally there are more sales in the first half of the calendar year since customers prefer to buy and move in the spring/summer months.

Applying a reasonable increase in sales over the previous equivalent half and perhaps also building in some modest increase in prices gives a projected turnover figure. This can then be extended for the second half using the same principles.

Combining the second half with the first half figure then gives the turnover projected for the year.

At the conclusion of that little exercise all the numbers should be scrutinised again – especially so if there is to be a further iteration of the forecast. Building projections on projections will multiply whatever errors are in the base projections.

The trap of spurious accuracy

One trap that everyone falls into when they begin to compile forecasts, is to forget about the implications of taking percentage increases in base figures.

By taking a percentage increase in a base value – say in average selling price – and then applying it without thinking can give some ludicrous results. Just because prices went up half-on-half by 4.76% does not mean that percentage should be applied unthinkingly into the future. *Either* use a sensible percentage increase (which might be defined as a single digit – so not three significant figures) *or* fix on a specific numerical value *rounded down* for safety.

As an illustration, if the ASP was, say, £345,000 in the base half and that represented a 5.3% increase over the previous equivalent half, then the total which is being projected for the subsequent half, should use *either* an uplift of 5% (that is, a similar uplift rounded down to a single digit) *or* a value of £362,000 (and not the £362,250 figure which a 'true' 5% increase would produce). The supposed accuracy of a projected number achieved by an unthinking application of a percentage merely looks ridiculous rather than sophisticated.

Forecasting to numbers less than a complete thousand just looks silly – especially the further into the future it goes – and indicates a lack of thought.

THE BASIC TECHNIQUE OF FORECASTING

The technique outlined above – of using two pieces of information to develop a third – is the process that is followed throughout the forecasting process.

If you were going to make a complete forecast for Barratt, you would now proceed by taking exactly the same principle to all the various components of the company's income statement. Costs are compared, category by category, with the equivalent period (and also the immediately preceding half year) to see what changes have occurred – *and what the trend is likely to be.*

The directors' reports are likely to be of great value here. The comments made in the narratives about individual operations may disclose certain important information about margins; cost reductions; headcount by operation or function; market conditions; and so on. All of these contribute to building up a picture of the changes (or stasis) in the components of cost.

A reasonable prediction is then made using this information and incorporated – category by category – into the projected income statement.

USING INFORMATION FROM OTHER ACCOUNTS SECTIONS

Some of the information has to be imported from other parts of the accounts where the crucial core information will be located. The state of the *balance sheet* at the end of last year compared with the interest charge for the first half can be used to see if borrowing has gone up or down or stayed the same (always adjusting for changes in underlying interest rates). The *Sources and Uses statement* will disclose whether the group/company was absorbing or throwing off cash at the last reported year. It will have shown if the company was shedding creditors; or reducing stocks; or having to build up its physical asset base, for instance. If it was absorbing cash (debt increasing) then, all other things being equal, the interest charge will increase. If it is generating cash (debt reducing) then – again all other things being equal – the interest charge for the year will probably fall.

This can then be used to produce a forecast of the interest charge that the company will face. But the interest charge need not be the same for both halves – the change from cash being generated to being absorbed can be very rapid as trading circumstances change.

All the time, while making predictions for individual components, information from the report has to be used to provide the basis for the forecasted elements and then these have to be compared against what the company has said in its report to see if they make sense and if they are realistic.

No one outside a company can forecast *exceptional or extraordinary items* – by definition – so these can be ignored in any prediction of profits. (Although it is possible that mention may be made at the 'half-way stage' when the interim results are published, in which case they should be taken into account.)

In the case of house-building companies, the forecast might be refined to some extent by using more of the information that the company provides in its full-year statement. This will include information about the regional mix of completions and prices and types of development.

For instance, if the company indicates that it intends to shift to building away from the South East in the next half-year then that might mean that prices per sold unit will drop – but equally margins per sold unit might rise. This might be because the costs of acquiring land are lower and the costs of employing skilled tradesmen are less outside the South East. If this were indicated, the analyst would have to fall back on historical information to try to work out what completions and margins might be – and make some educated guesses about the consequences.

Similar changes might happen for other companies in other sectors but the magnitude and direction of the changes will depend upon the characteristics of the individual company and the industry it is located in.

When forecasting half-by-half, it is important not to forget to add together the two halves to calculate the full-year effect. And if the first-half projection indicates that the usage of cash is diminishing or increasing particularly fast, then that effect also has to be extended into the second half – and consequently the complete year.

Similarly, fixed and variable costs do not have to be identical half by half – sometimes a dramatic change in these can be the cause of a major shift in profitability, as the company sheds costs more rapidly than anticipated or perhaps has to take on costs that were otherwise unforeseen.

ITERATION – AGAIN!

Once the individual components have been forecast, the numbers are totted up to give a pre-tax figure. It should be at this point that the overall forecast is evaluated for reasonableness.

Sometimes individual movements in components look right but when they are aggregated, the small changes that have been made in each produce a cumulative result that is obviously wrong.

If it looks wrong then it probably is wrong. The forecasted total then has to be changed by tweaking individual components until it does look right. This also has to be done with regard to the split between halves of the year – so it can be a difficult (and tedious) process to get right. But unless it is as right as the analyst can get it – both in a year-on-year sense and in a year-by-year sense – then it will be worthless as a forecast.

Arriving at the pre-tax figure is almost the culmination of the exercise, but since share price movements are driven by the relationship between the earnings and the share price itself, it is necessary to forecast the earnings that the pre-tax figure produces.

Because of the difficulties and complexities of the tax charge, most analysts adopt a standard tax charge based on the prevailing corporation tax rate. This 'standard' tax charge is applied to the pre-tax number – using the prevailing corporation tax rate – and then dividing the result by the average number of shares that are forecast to be in issue in the year to come.

Calculating the future earnings per share

The actual rate of tax that a company's profits bear is a composite that is impossible to accurately forecast from outside the company so almost all analysis uses a standard rate to equalise the calculation between companies and put them all on the same footing.

If, for some reason, the company is a persistent beneficiary of a low tax charge and this is likely to continue into the future, it might be permissible to use a historic charge in calculating the future earnings. If this is done it must be noted in any published forecast (that is, a forecast where more than one person is party to the information that is being used). But this still risks a very odd result being calculated that is far outside the market range of PEs and therefore likely to make the shares look spuriously cheap or expensive.

For simplicity, the average number of shares that are *forecast* to be in issue is mostly likely to be the number that were in issue at the year end – but sometimes companies give advance warning of their intentions to issue more, or a share issue made just after the year end crystallises or perhaps there is a buying programme to reduce the number of shares in issue. All of these would have to be taken into account.

CHAPTER 10

The Sources and Uses – predicting future finance use

Share price movements

The tripod

Crucial questions on assumptions

Following through on the logic of the forecast Income Statement

Consistency and iteration

Using all the information available

Composite values

SHARE PRICE MOVEMENTS

Since share prices move mostly on changes in earnings per share, a beginner might be forgiven for thinking that once the estimate of future profit has been completed, the job of forecasting is over. Based on anticipated profits, earnings per share can be calculated; the future level of profit can then be compared with the current level, with the market average and with specific alternatives like other companies. A strategy can be put in place for buying, selling or just watching the way that the share price moves. All of that is true, of course, but not *all* of the job has been done. In order to complete the task, an *integrated forecast* has to be made which involves all the elements of the accounts – not just the income statement but the S&U and the balance sheet too.

THE TRIPOD

This is because the validity of the forecast can only be tested if the other two legs of the tripod – the sources and uses of funds and the balance sheet – are also forecast, using the same assumptions about what will happen to the company. If this is not done then the predicted level of income and resultant level of earnings are left hanging in the air, unsupported by the verifying assumptions that underpin the structure of the company's finances. The rule of three again.

Some assumptions might have been included in the profit forecast which will also affect the company's ability to generate cash; or might require the company to take on more debt or to change its working capital targets. In order to be sure about the validity of the forecast income statement, the predicted changes have to be thought through for their impact on both the S&U and the balance sheet.

A forecast prepared without the benefit of testing the underlying assumptions through constructing a forecast balance sheet, and a forecast sources and uses, *may* be right but it may also have left out some crucial underlying changes in the company's financial skeleton – and these will undermine the reasonableness of the predictions.

CRUCIAL QUESTIONS ON ASSUMPTIONS

Questions that the analysts should ask as the prediction process proceeds might include the following:

- Can sales be expanded without increasing stock levels? If stock levels are expanded, what is the cost of the change in working capital?

- Can receivables be dragged in to help finance the level of stocks required?

- If not how might the company's borrowings be affected?

- Can extra sales be generated only by allowing margins to deteriorate (perhaps by reducing prices or extending credit)?

- If this is the case, what will happen to debtors and creditors (receivables and payables) and how does that then go back to affect finance charges and profitability?

These questions —and similar ones about the financial mechanics of the sales generation process which will help to support the sense of the profit forecast – can be partially answered by seeing what the effect of the assumptions made about the income statement have upon the S&U and the balance sheet in the year(s) ahead.

FOLLOWING THROUGH ON THE LOGIC OF THE FORECAST INCOME STATEMENT

The process for constructing a projected S&U is less computational than the process of forecasting the income statement. It is essentially more conceptual, in that the trends which underlie the forecast for the Income Statement have to be carried into the S&U – but without necessarily being ascribed (initially) concrete values.

Often the numerical relationships which might be inferred from an examination of the income statements of past years – margins are x% of turnover; costs are y% of turnover; interest costs are lower in the second half of the year and so on – cannot be transferred over into movements in the S&U. If there are relationships then they are often not directly evident from an examination of the S&U in comparison with the income statement, or cannot be given a concrete relationship of the type 'if x, then y'.

The analyst's job then becomes one of trying to ascribe reasonable values to the components of the S&U in the light of experience – or the reasonableness of the assumptions that were employed.

In some cases it is possible to 'model' a company's finances as an outsider. At the time when the house-building industry was very much more buoyant than it is now, in the third quarter of the twentieth century for instance (private 'completions' reached over 220,000 per annum in the late 1960s), the building materials industry – especially brick-making businesses and cement manufacturers –

used to have a pattern of trading that was fairly responsive to changes in the level of building activity.

Some companies – which no longer exist as separate businesses – used to specialise in manufacturing types of brick ('stock' or 'architecturals' or 'engineering') or had dominance of regional markets (because of the high cost to value of transporting bricks local sources of supply were often favoured). With regional levels of house-building activity also being amenable to prediction (because of the larger number involved), it became possible to construct financial models that produced reasonably accurate forecasts of profits for individual building materials companies.

These would take into account factors such as transport costs; energy price changes; labour charges; and inflation as well as the changes in activity and market share brought about by competitor activity, changes in product range and architectural tastes.

The inability of producers to alter production levels rapidly and dramatically (because of production constraints concerning the use of kilns) and changes in building activity then allowed alert analysts to make reasonable stabs at producing conceptual models of a company's production profile that could then be fed back into estimates of stock-holding, debtor and creditor movements, and working capital requirements, as new information was released on a quarterly basis about housing starts.

These would then, in their turn, affect the forecasts of profit as the costs of stockholding were taken into account or the benefits of selling from stock were fed into the forecasts.

(Some analysts even used to take frequent trips past brickyards to make their own visual assessments of the level of stockholdings, in the light of their experience of what they were 'normally' at the same time a year or two years ago. This is no longer so easily accomplished for the building sector because of all the structural changes that have occurred in the industry as well as the decline in the level of house-building. Even so, some very experienced analysts will still be able to draw on a long experience of the industry to identify key correlations between external activity and financial changes).

CONSISTENCY AND ITERATION

The point about tying the S&U into the conceptual framework of the Income Statement is that it forces the analyst to think about the realism of the concepts and assumptions underlying the forecast values that have been included in the predicted Income Statement. While these may not produce testable and verifiable numerical relationships, the soundness of the assumptions will become apparent through the process of trying to make numerical changes in the individual components of the S&U which reflect the changes and assumptions that have been used in producing a forecast for the Income Statement.

If the analyst has decided that turnover is going to increase, then certain consequences flow from that. Expanded turnover means that stocks usually have to rise in anticipation; debtor levels may extend both absolutely and in terms of payment days; creditor patterns will also alter.

Some or all of these will have to be taken into account in producing an *integrated forecast* for the company. Looking at the pattern of change in the financing of a business over a period of years, as revealed by the changes in the S&U, as turnover expanded or contracted, profits went up or down and the level of economic activity changed will eventually produce a 'feel' for how one will change as a consequence of a change in the other.

Cash as a component

Cash is one of the raw materials of businesses, just like physical raw materials, labour and machinery. So it is almost impossible to conceive of expansion of a business without an additional injection of cash from somewhere. The issue is whether this injection can be generated by the business itself.

Sometimes because of the terms of trade of the products and services offered, companies are able to generate their own cash to enable expansion. Sometimes expansion can be achieved by running down an existing cash pile or by gradually matching modest increases in margin with the physical resources required for a subsequent and larger expansion in turnover. Sometimes shareholders have to be asked to contribute; sometimes bank debt can fuel expansion. Occasionally, customers and suppliers can be manipulated to help. Whichever of the routes chosen, it should be obvious that some change in working capital takes place when a business makes a positive (or negative) change in its level of activity. The critical changes are therefore among the components of working capital – in receivables (debtors), payables (creditors) and stock.

This boils down to the simple assertion that what analysts are trying to do when they forecast the S&U is to forecast changes in working capital. Looked at from this single viewpoint, the forecasting process probably becomes less daunting.

USING ALL THE INFORMATION AVAILABLE

Absolute accuracy in predicting the movements in stocks, debtors or creditors is *not* the target. Rather, the aim of the exercise is to make sure that the trends in the movements of the working capital components are properly reflected in the thinking about what happens to the income statement (and then what is going to happen to the balance sheet). All the elements of the accounts interact with each other – so to leave two unadjusted after one has been altered obviously makes no sense. It could be positively damaging to the integrity of the forecasts.

The process of triangulation of each of the three parts of the accounting tripod, one with another, to ensure verification, *requires* that the other two parts of the structure be adjusted if any one of them is altered.

COMPOSITE VALUES

One further wrinkle needs to be smoothed out.

Working capital is a *portfolio concept* – a composite value. It is the sum of movements in debtors, creditors and stocks. Since it is a summative value

– the product of three separate elements – it does not necessarily have to be the case that all of these are moving in the same direction. The analyst has to be careful that the correct directions of movements have been incorporated into the final forecast. Again, the precise values – while they are important to the numerical calculation – are of less importance than the consistency of thinking that supports the forecast.

A critical evaluation of the movements in the S&U should be the final step in the process – an iterative mechanism to ensure that the thinking behind the changes in the S&U are carried through into the completion of the forecast of the Income Statement, with any adjustments being made to the S&U if there is seen to be an incongruity between the two.

Every time the S&U is changed then the income statement has to be checked again and, if necessary, final tweaks made to the S&U values as a consequence.

CHAPTER 11

The Balance Sheet – the effect of the structure on company finances

Bringing all the information together

Consistency and uniformity of assumptions

Simultaneous entry

Check! Check! Check!

BRINGING ALL THE INFORMATION TOGETHER

It should now be completely transparent that the balance sheet is both affected by and has an effect on the income statement.

If this is accepted as being axiomatic, then as a final measure to complete the forecasting process, it is obviously necessary to ensure that a (predicted) balance sheet is congruent with the predicted income statement and predicted S&U. This has to be the case given the exigencies of financial triangulation and the obligation to ensure that changes in one financial component are carried through into the other two.

CONSISTENCY AND UNIFORMITY OF ASSUMPTIONS

The thinking that underpins forecasts in any one part of the accounts has to be absolutely consistent with what happens in the other two. The only effective way of doing this is to follow the process of forecasting through to make consistent – and mutually supportive – changes in *all* the elements.

A case might be made that if the StRuGL is left out of this process then the 'completion' argument is not being followed through to its logical conclusion.

There is some validity to this. But the internal consistency of the income statement, the S&U and the balance sheet are not dependent upon the StRuGL – which is a derived document. If the StRuGL were absolutely critical as one of the legs of the accounts then, of course, it would be necessary to complete a forecast of that too.

As it is without a crucial role of importance in proving the others, that goes beyond triangulation and into a fourth dimension of verification. As such it is superfluous.

A further check on the consistency of the forecasts *might*, in some circumstances, be achieved by looking at the StRuGL to ensure that summative changes are properly reflected in it, but this is essentially for those of a 'completist' bent only – or the sort of people who enjoy bending their minds playing three-dimensional chess.

A NAGGING AND LAGGING ISSUE

The balance sheet is the first document to be created in accounting terms – the primary one for control purposes – and yet is the last to be used in the forecasting period. Why should this be so?

The answer lies in two reasons – chronology and development. First, the balance sheet changes (in normal circumstances) only as a result of changes in trading during some period; the income statement is what drives changes in the balance sheet in that period.

Second, these changes are reflected in the sources and uses.

Think of a speeded-up movie film of a plant growing and developing. The first, establishing shot shows the plant as it is: a small stalk, a few leaves and maybe some flower buds. That is the balance sheet in the first period.

As the film progresses, leaves whirl about and grow; tendrils from the stalk shoot out to support further growth; blossoms burst open and attract insects – these might be thought of as the plant's customers. These actions, showing the development of the plant, are like the Sources and Uses statement. They show the detail of changes in the structure of the plant and how they came about.

The final, concluding shot shows the plant as it now is after the changes have all occurred. This is the balance sheet again – at the end of the second period.

That little excursion into the world of nature films should also point up a further issue. The film could be stopped *anywhere* in time and the plant would have developed in line with the changes that were shown: the Sources and Uses shows what happens during that period but the changes can only be summed up at the end of the period – whatever that may be.

(To extend the analogy further, a list could be made of the inputs and outputs of the plant – so much water absorbed; so many hours of sunlight; so much nutrient taken up. In return the plant gained additional height; grew x number of flowers; lost y number and produced z number of new buds or fruits. That summation would be comparable to the Income Statement.)

SIMULTANEOUS ENTRY

The best and safest way of calculating the shape of the new balance sheet is to undertake the work simultaneously with the calculation of the projected S&U. That way thinking again becomes self-checking and the danger of making errors in transcription – as changed values in any one component are altered in the others – is minimised.

Every time that a change is thought of and justified in the S&U it is entered – or at least noted alongside the appropriate line – simultaneously into the old balance sheet values to give (eventually, when all the changes have been made) the new forecast balance sheet. Unless there have been very substantial changes in the forecast income statement, then the balance sheet will probably only display modest changes. If it does not – and the changes look very large – then probably something has been forecast unreasonably.

One of the best ways to perform checks on the forecast balance sheet is to compute the same ratios that were looked at on the original balance sheet – gearing; stock ratio; quick ratio and so on – and see if they have changed very markedly (more than 10%, say). If they have then it is worth going back and reviewing the changes that have been made in both the other components (S&U and income statement) and seeing if anything looks wrong. If it does, necessary corrections will have to be made.

Furthermore since the balance sheet *must* balance at the end of the exercise, by making the changes this way, it becomes easier to ensure consistency between the Income Statement changes, the S&U changes and the projected balance sheet. Making all the changes in the balance sheet *concurrently* with the changes that are being made in the S&U ensures that reasons are self-justified; values are thought through; and nothing is left out.

CHECK! CHECK! CHECK!

Particular attention should be paid to the company's forecast cash position. In many ways, cash on a projected balance sheet is the *balancing item* – the element that can be adjusted to make sure that the whole thing balances. However, it is all too easy to use this item to cover up errors in other parts of the projections – brought about either through internal inconsistencies in the projections or through lazy and uncompleted logic.

For instance, if a forecast is made which suggests that sales are going to expand rapidly then, all other things being equal, cash holdings will not increase in the same year. Or if the company is experiencing difficult market conditions in advancing sales, cash will probably reduce. The permutations of all these possible trading factors are far too many to enumerate. The analyst has to apply common sense principles to see if the projections that have been prepared are both reasonable *and* internally consistent.

CHAPTER 12

A summary of 'Red Flags'

Understanding the term

The incidence of red flag issues – where they come from

    Turnover

    Matching profits and costs; accounting policies

    Margins

    Costs

    Interest charges

    Auditors

    Stocks

    Working capital generally

    Cash

    Uncovered dividends

UNDERSTANDING THE TERM

Many reports on companies, and some academic textbooks, refer to so-called 'red flags' – the expression that they use to indicate that there is something that needs to be investigated further about issues of interpretation in a set of accounts. Some analysts might take this further and suggest that their existence is sufficiently significant to preclude taking the company's financial position as secure.

Though the term is prevalent in textbooks and in academic teaching, there is no common definition for 'red flags' in accounting terms. It can almost mean what the user wants it to mean – anything from a gentle 'Look out' to the imperative of 'Go no further'. But the basic concept of a red flag indicating some form of warning is well understood.

Although most red flag issues will have been covered in the appropriate chapters on the components of the accounts already, a summary of the major incidences is set out here, for convenience.

The list is not supposed to be fully comprehensive or complete, as individual company circumstances will affect the way that the accounts have to be interpreted and red flags will therefore have a shape-shifting character. Sometimes issues that are completely innocent in both theory and for one set of a company's accounts will assume a more ambiguous caste when seen in the context of other factors.

These other factors may equally be innocent in themselves but become ambiguous in combination. Collective and combinatory evidence has to be considered in all forms of financial investigation, as well as individual instances of warnings.

In every case, the common characteristic is a *divergence* from either historical patterns or from market-place orthodoxy. It is this divergence that needs to be held constantly in mind and each factor of the accounts has to be examined against the run of historical data or common conditions for other similar businesses.

The best way to summarise potential red flag issues is to list them in the way that they might probably arise on an examination of a set of accounts – starting with the Income Statement, moving on to the balance sheet and ending up with the Sources and Uses.

THE INCIDENCE OF RED FLAG ISSUES – WHERE THEY COME FROM

Turnover

The natural progression of turnover is upwards. Most businesses expect turnover to grow at least annually – possibly even every half year. (Certainly this is the case with publicly listed companies; private companies might have other considerations.)

Shareholders in public companies would expect to see annual increases in profits, in order to propel annual increases in dividends. So most analysts will expect to see an increase in turnover year on year supporting an increase in profits, which translates into higher earnings per share and then into a higher share price.

Turnover which does *not grow* may signal something which should be investigated further – it may be the start of a long-term decline in a market place or a product range. Or, of course, it may be nothing more than a temporary blip.

Finding out which it is can be done by delving more deeply into the rest of the accounts – and particularly the narrative explanations given in the directors' report section and perhaps in response to questioning or financial commentaries.

But turnover which is *growing too fast* can also indicate some form of problem which needs to be considered. It may give a clue to policies run by the company: Is turnover being bought at the expense of margins? Is it soundly based in accounting terms? Have accounting policies changed to produce different results from those previously?

Turnover which experiences no real annual fluctuation may also be an indication of something being wrong. Many years ago a company called Acrow, which specialised in construction machinery, allegedly recorded twenty-three years of unbroken profits – in one of the more volatile of the industrial sectors. This was a feat that appeared to defy gravity. The company was eventually brought to earth after a sustained period of reversal in the construction business worldwide when it was no longer able to perpetrate the same accounting device it had relied on for so many years.

Acrow's accounting camouflage

Using its worldwide network of associates, each financial year the parent company had been pushing stock out to companies which were in areas not in recession just before its own year end and then buying it back and redistributing it across the globe as individual areas recovered or dipped, in the new financial year.

So there were vast amounts of construction equipment perpetually in motion across the globe – all of which had been the output of the listed UK company in the previous year. Since the companies participating in this accounting sleight of hand were all associated with Acrow rather than being owned outright, it did not have to consolidate their results in its own accounts and so managed to maintain the fiction of consistently increasing profits until the worldwide recession of the 1980s pushed everywhere down at the same time.

Sadly, many commentators in the financial media and analysts in broking houses knew about the company's practices and did not care to make the illusion known to the investing public, preferring to shelter behind the fig leaf offered by the fact this practice was a mere warping of the then-operative accounting rules rather than an outright fracture of them.

What is less obviously considered is the *composition* of turnover. Although there may be a superficially similar result, the substitution of more, but lower-margin products for fewer higher-margin ones will result in turnover that may be sustained. But eventually these may have different rates of progress in turnover growth. Such substitutions may also indicate what is happening to the company in the market place.

Matching profits and costs; accounting policies

In calculating the profit on long-term projects, accountants are supposed to only take profits when foreseeable costs have been fully provided for. They are also supposed match costs against turnover (in timing terms) and to exercise prudence throughout.

All these activities require the application of judgement – which is, of course, a very subjective thing. It goes without saying, then, that it is possible for even honest men to disagree over when and how profits may be taken on long-term projects.

The company's accounting policies are supposed to disclose the way in which this is done. But the statement may be anodyne and disclose very little – in which case it should be compared with a statement from a company in a similar line of business to see if more light can be shed. This might then yield a pale-red flag.

A vivid-red flag would be flung up if a company's accounting policies changed substantially and frequently.

Margins

Declining margins are never a good thing – and if unsupported by a narrative explanation may indicate a serious problem which the company management is unwilling to countenance publicly. But margins are not static and a judicious view should be taken about temporary falls from previous year. Far more worrying are margins consistently *higher than the market average* or which look 'odd' in some way.

Interpreting information correctly, as an outsider, is often a matter of taking imaginative leaps, using firm evidence as the jumping-off platform. So an intuition that something looks odd may well be a valid prompt to investigate further, simply because it jibes with what could reasonably – intuitively – be expected. Margins which are always higher than those achieved by other companies are *not* normal, since the market always tends to a self-levelling position. They usually indicate some form of liberties being taken with statistical records and are certainly worth studying further. (The cases of Sino-Forest and Parmalat, dealt with in the next chapter, both came to light partly because of gravity-defying margins which could not be adequately explained otherwise.)

Costs

Costs which never appear to change may be the precursor of some significant problem just as the continuous usage of exceptional costs may well be an attempt by managers to conceal some deep-rooted problem that continually affects profitability.

Interest charges

Interest charges different from what might have been expected are always worth investigating more. One of four reasons is likely:

- The analyst has wrongly estimated the interest charge on the (correct) balances.

- The debt has grown faster or diminished faster than the analyst allowed.

- There is a substantial intra-year variation in debt not allowed for by the analyst.

- Someone in the company has cooked the books – usually by just moving debt 'off balance sheet'; for examples of this see the next chapter.

Auditors

Auditors are supposed to catch such malpractice, of course. But the record of the large auditing companies is nothing to boast about (see the list of audit and accounting failures in Appendix Two) and small audit firms often lack the technical resources to undertake the policing role that has been pushed on them. Furthermore, despite the supposed universality of accounting regulations, cultural differences often impinge on the overall standard of internationally based companies, with lots of audits conducted in different countries.

Auditors being frequently changed or with too long a relationship with their audit clients may also be taken as a potential red flag – not deepest-red perhaps but pretty heavily tinged.

In the balance sheet the major areas for some form of 'misunderstanding' are:

Stocks

As the next chapter will show in more detail, one of Bloomfield's laws states that 'every number greater than one is a liar' in accounting terms and nowhere more so than in the tricky problem of assigning value to stocks. This can allow great latitude to unscrupulous managers and is often very difficult to detect. What has to be allowed for is that it is often a system failure that allows a junior manager to distort stock or working capital rather than an action emanating from the top of the company. Such distortions often occur to protect a job incumbent from an investigation; to hide a shortfall in profitability or a targeted level of turnover; or to cover up a quality problem.

Such system failures can be very difficult to disentangle from the normal run of business. Often the people best placed to manipulate systems are those most closely concerned with them. Because of this, deep-seated failures of systems are usually only revealed when some other problem also occurs to interfere with the smooth operation of the fraud – when the wave goes out suddenly, you can see who hasn't been wearing swimming trunks!

Working capital generally

The close inter-relationship between debtor balances, creditor balances and stock in manufacturing businesses allows the manager who is disposed to cheat considerable leeway in 'teeming and lading' accounting reports.

Cash

Cash balances rarely lie. It is very difficult to muck about with cash. In fact, cash is usually the tell-tale indicator that helps to disclose problems elsewhere. When cash looks badly out of kilter with the needs or performance of the business then there is almost always something wrong – although it may be the analyst at fault, of course, in the same way as with interest charges (see above).

In those occasions when problems are later disclosed to have affected cash balances (as with the Satyam case in India or the Parmalat case in Italy), it can only have been because the auditors were lax or complicit with management in their erroneous tallying of cash balances.

In the sources and uses of funds statement, there is usually little that will spring out at the analyst as being manifestly wrong – the more likely places for error are in the income statement and the balance sheet. The S&U is merely a synthesis of the other two so it is very unlikely that it will contain anything novel or visibly odd that will not have already been spotted.

What it can do is alert the analyst to some feature that may have been visible before, through a close inspection of the income statement or the balance sheet, but may have not been quite as stark as when the S&U emphasises it.

This will usually be the case with stock changes or with one of the other working capital components.

Uncovered dividends

There is one final red flag that doesn't really fit into these categories completely comfortably – the issue of uncovered *dividends*. It is possible for a company to pay out dividends beyond the amount it has earned in post-tax profits (see Chapter Two) if there are distributable reserves from which to do so. But consistently paying out more than it has earned is a very imprudent policy for a company and suggests that the unpleasant decision to cut the rate of dividend payment is being put off. A company whose depressed share price is the cause of a *very high yield* is also a flag to the effect that the market believes that the coming dividend is ripe for cutting.

The general rule about 'red flag' issues is that they are usually the product of some divergence from the expected. The analyst always has to guard against a self-induced error in forecasting but if this is eliminated, anything that remains is worthy of some form of comment – either in 'note to self' form or, when all other possibilities have been actively eliminated, in a more public indication of concern.

PART FOUR

MOSTLY MISCHIEF

CHAPTER 13

Accounting Mischief – the theory

Most accounts are valid

The five methods of altering accounts

The point of application

The income statement

The balance sheet

Chapters Nine, Ten and Eleven dealt with the application of simple analytical techniques to enable the projection of company financial information to help make reasonable forecasts of profitability and financial strength. Investment decisions about which company to invest in can then be based on such projections.

MOST ACCOUNTS ARE VALID

The examples of analysis have been contained to instances where – although the information may require some investigation to get hold of – the processes are largely straightforward and the outcomes are not likely to be affected by the original source information being anything other than properly prepared, correctly audited and honestly reported.

This is a reasonable position to take for understanding accounts since the vast majority of listed companies (in the UK at least) are run honestly and properly, with no more of the inefficiency than is normally to be expected in human affairs.

However, every so often a corporate scandal breaks which reveals how easy it is to part investors from their money, using manipulated information, modest deception or outright and completely intentional fraud.

In recent years this appears to have happened with increasing frequency as sometimes misguided, but more usually unscrupulous, dishonest individuals have been found out after the discovery of frauds that they originated or perpetuated.

These have usually been designed to enrich the perpetrators at the expense of others, either directly through taking money from the gullible (like the fraudulent investment 'Ponzi' schemes run by the American Bernie Madoff) – or indirectly through manipulating company information to maintain or inflate share prices from which the perpetrators have benefitted personally. These people will have been the beneficiaries of either unearned bonuses or inflated salaries or the unjustified continued occupation of positions of corporate power.

Such activity is often given the name *'creative accounting'* – an intended irony because it uses the information available to the accountant to create a picture that is *close* to the truth but *not completely* the truth, which benefits those preparing it.

The first thing to appreciate in thinking about the issues involved in 'creative accounting' is *Bloomfield's First Law* (which I just invented), which states that

'In accounting terms any number greater than one is a liar.'

This gives the logical foundation for the information to be presented the way it is – even if that logic is distorted.

The elaboration of the bald and counter-intuitive statement that some numbers lie – in fact all numbers after the very first one – is based on the concept that the process of accounting is not simply about dealing with *quantities* but also dealing with *time*. So what may appear to be a discrete quantity when it is left by itself, untainted by the passage of time, becomes something more complicated with the issue of when it was used or accounted for, taken into consideration.

To take a very simple example, as an instance, a one-man business operating in discrete time periods will have quite uncomplicated accounting needs. If a potter buys clay and uses it all to produce one pot, which he sells immediately after firing it and then makes no more during the course of the year, living on the proceeds of the one pot, the accounting is fairly simple and intuitive.

But if he buys enough clay for several pots, lasting him long enough to make five pots in one year and then a further four the subsequent year, and if he sells three pots in the first year having made three and a half (having left one ready to fire just as the financial year ended – so half a completed pot) and if he then makes two and a half in the second (two new ones and completing the half-finished one) and sells a further four in the year after that (when he has made no more pots but using up all his clay), then the accounting for those is obviously a lot more complicated about what the stock values and profits really are.

To choose exactly what the accounting values are for stock, profit and income is quite complicated and open to some judgement rather than to absolute certainty. It is this latitude over the values of discrete items which gives the room for the creative accountant to exercise imagination.

In this chapter six examples will be looked at in detail to provide some pointers to what goes on in such misrepresentations and illusions on which they rest. This is quite a long chapter in consequence; it is broken down into sections that deal with illustrations of the various techniques that have been used. This comes after some general theoretical points which highlight the mischief that can be wrought by those who want to bend the principle of proper accounting for their own devices.

The list of corporate frauds and scandals – never mind less-serious examples of interpretation – that could have provided examples, is very long. It goes back at least to the seventeenth century – the time of the Dutch tulip riots. For British readers the foremost historical example is the infamous English South Sea Company, formed in the eighteenth century for 'an undertaking of Great Advantage but no one to know what it is' as the Memorandum of Association described it (which should have been warning enough).

Shelves of books have been written about such scams (fictional, factual and a blend of both). There is material on scams, frauds and the use of creative accounting for many interesting hours of reading – not least because the number of books has increased as the number of scams has increased in recent years. (A list of some of the scandals in accounting or financial manipulation in the UK is given at Appendix One, for the period which represented roughly the high point of the cult of 'shareholder value'.)

It might be thought that the thicket of current accounting rules should prevent such misbehaviour – especially as the density and complexity of those rules, which are supposed to bind accountants' individual practices to a uniform set of techniques, increase annually. Unfortunately this is not the case – for two principal reasons.

First, at least as much intellectual effort will be applied in out-witting the rules as in applying them. This is the case with every accounting rule ever invented and is sometimes due to good intentions (to try to resolve ambiguities in the specific application of rules) but is often attributable to purely base motives (to evade the application of rules for some personal or corporate benefit, which then translates into a personal benefit).

Second, scandals break out where there is a failure of the reach of good corporate governance and the rules of accounting to meet and mesh. These are very common. As rules get collectively more complicated, so the area of their application and the overlap among them gets more difficult to interpret, sometimes leaving gaps in the apparent coverage.

Just as weeds flourish in the cracks between paving stones, so fraud and deception take root where accounting and governance rules are overlapping or incomplete (despite their apparent complexity).

Despite the protestations of the regulators, the professions and company directors, standards of UK corporate governance are underwhelming. Among the individuals who head companies there are some who are unusually over-bearing and arrogant, with characteristics akin to the psychopathic, who routinely attempt to justify instances of behaviour that the 'rules' supposedly prohibit – and usually do so as being 'in the interests of shareholders'.

It is during the tenure of these individuals that scandals often occur. In the UK these have included the numerous scandals involving banks manipulating exchange and interest rates (especially at Barclays and RBS); the selling of worthless insurance (Lloyds, in particular); the creation of corporate targets that are so high they cannot be achieved (Tesco); the attempts to supercharge company results by ludicrous financial engineering (Mitchells and Butler); and the deliberate concealment of bribe payments on a massive scale (BAe). These are just a few examples taken from a much more extensive list.

The standards of corporate governance outside the jurisdiction of the UK are, if anything, even worse. *Every* country in Europe, in the Americas, in Africa and in Asia has reported instances of accounting scandals – greater or lesser. Some of the largest and most familiar among international firms have been tainted by accounting scandals – and some more than once.

So the purpose of understanding and analysing accounts is not simply to be able to create projections on which to base a decision about investment but also to help sort out the sheep from the goats (of which there appears to be an increasing number being smuggled into the flock).

Unfortunately the brainpower and effort devoted to evading the accounting rules is the equal of that employed in devising and enforcing them, so even the most skilled analyst/interpreters will not see though the smoke either every time or the first time.

What usually brings scams and scandals to the light of day is that any attempt to conceal or manipulate information requires increasing amounts of effort and more and more elaborate facades to be created as time goes on. These then get stretched and stretched to the point of flimsiness.

Astute analysis undertaken over a period of time will inevitably begin to reveal the tears in the corporate accounting fabric as the truth is stretched ever thinner to its eventual breaking point. It eventually becomes very difficult to maintain the illusion and analysis of the consistency and congruence of the accounting information begins to reveal disparities between what is being presented and the truth.

THE FIVE METHODS OF ALTERING ACCOUNTS

Until the arrival of one of the companies whose stories are recounted below, traditional accounting wisdom held that there were only four major methods of constructing accounting information that misrepresented the correct position:

- Maximise turnover
- Minimise costs
- Increase assets
- Decrease liabilities

Everything else might be considered to be a variant of these methods. However, it might be suggested that with the mega-fraud represented by Enron, trickster accountants developed a fifth device – that is, eliminating some information that is not supportive of the company's case by

- Pushing information completely out of the purview of the accounts.

The justification for this claim of a new category of trickery is that the scale of the exercise in the Enron case was so vast.

How this is done is examined below in the brief descriptions of a few examples selected from the last twenty years, set out below. In the next chapter some more detailed information is given of how accounts were distorted in specific cases.

Maximising income

- The *Satyam* scandal from India – an example of inflated invoices (and invented bank movements). Founded in 1987, Satyam eventually became the (supposedly) fourth-ranked company in the IT sector in India, dealing particularly with out-sourced computing and data management. That was until its share price collapsed in 2008 when the founder eventually had to confess that he had been inventing revenue for almost the entire life of the business.

- Toshiba's inflation of its turnover and sales figures, fully revealed in Japan in the summer of 2015, following on from the similar Olympus scandal that came to light five years previously. This was a case of hubris brought about by a treadmill of internally/centrally generated trading forecasts that simply could not be achieved.

Minimising costs

- This is what *Tesco* appears to have done over a prolonged period, probably from the start of the twenty-first century. The detail of this case is considered more fully in the next chapter – within the limits available, given that it is the subject of an investigation at the time of writing.

Increasing assets

- The *Sino-Forest* affair – an example of a Chinese company listed on the Toronto Stock Exchange which involved negligible regulatory oversight and the creation of imaginary assets on the grand scale; this case is covered extensively in the next chapter.

- *Royal Dutch Shell* chose to inflate the value (by inflating the economic life) of its oilfields and was found out in 2004. This appears to have been the result of a power struggle in the company as much as anything else.

Decreasing liabilities

- Usually this is accomplished by extending the life of liabilities – so pushing them beyond the annual accounting horizon. *Parmalat* used this method when it reclassified debt as equity – pushing the horizon for maturity of the financing instruments out to infinity, since equity *never* has to be repaid. The misbehaviour at this company is one of the examples considered in more detail in the next chapter.

Eliminating information

- The *Enron* scandal, and collapse, in the USA – which illustrates the use of 'off-balance sheet' devices to conceal crucial structural information.

- The Parmalat Affair from Italy – which employed all of the devices and techniques of concealment, elimination, flattery and invention at some point and therefore required the collusion of the auditors (or took advantage of their incompetence).

Why such behaviour occurs requires a different classification and set of explanations. The principal reasons can be classified as:

1. Personal gain

2. Meeting market expectations

3. Covering up fraud

Occasionally it is also for reasons of

4. corporate survival

- In highly regulated industries – the financial sector used to be a good example but fraudulent practices seems to have spread wider – some companies manipulate their earnings so as to fend off interference by the authorities.

- Asset values might be manipulated so as not to breach debt covenants – but this probably usually happens in private companies outside the realm of the public market.

However, mischief is usually done to benefit managers in some way – that is for personal gain, either actual or deferred:

- Smoothing profits so investors believe that the company is more stable and hence safer as an investment; allowing the managers both to retain their jobs and push for higher salaries and bonuses.

- Meeting annual earnings forecasts to convince the market the company managers know what they are doing.

- Manipulating earnings to receive higher bonuses (although this has now become less significant in recent years as company remuneration committees appear to have become willing to take managers' sides over the shareholders if targets are missed or a mixed set of targets is used, some of which are achieved and some not).

- Decreasing the record of a previous set of managers, after a forced change, so as to enhance the new incumbents' apparent record.

- Swelling earnings just before a share issue, to enhance the price at which they are issued.

- Inflating earnings just before an acquisition so as to have suffer less dilution when new shares are issued (since fewer higher-priced shares have to be issued if the deal is a mix of shares and cash or on an all-share basis).

- And so on and so on . . .

These actions usually involve not simply distorting or fabricating the numbers in the accounts but also the narratives that accompany them. The careful choice of words can disguise partially corrupt information as well as reveal the true picture.

The methods by which such mischief can be accomplished are many and only limited by the imagination and technical skill of the miscreant – although the more complicated ones require collaboration with, and the complicity of, other accountants, managers, auditors and lawyers. When mischief occurs in a company's accounting function it is rarely limited to one individual – as well as personality factors, the culture of the business has a great deal of influence on what happens, how it happens and why it happens.

THE POINT OF APPLICATION

A small library of books has been written about accounting scandals – some of these are quite racy and some are meant just for technical consumption. A brief list for further reading for those interested is given at Appendix Three.

Mostly, the places where the damage is done are the income statement and the balance sheet. The sources and uses of funds has to be manipulated to make everything agree but is not generally the *locus* of the problem. Some instances of how this can be done are given below.

The Income Statement

Outside of outright fabrication of numbers, the scope for improving profits lies mostly in terms of the point – *the timing* – at which costs are recognised. The issue of valuing long-term contracts has already been touched on.

Judgement is required by both managers and accountants in deciding when and how costs should be allocated to a project lasting several years and although the accounting regulations provide a guide, a certain amount of judicious interpretation is still required.

Sliding the costs around the contract even very slightly can be a significant source of profit generation – not overall, of course, since if all the costs are properly accounted for then the profits have to be what they are.

But by retarding or advancing costs slightly, it may be possible to smooth profits slightly or to hold back profits to be reported on an otherwise rainy day for the share price.

Overhead costs

These are supposed to be included in stock calculations and when these stocks are used in producing goods for sale, the profitability can obviously be affected. By tinkering slightly with when and how overheads are charged, profits can be affected – positively or negatively. This, again, can be used to affect the trend-line of profitability, depending on how the company is performing overall. It may be 'right' to advance costs in good years to provide for some reserve when things are not so good, for instance. This would be held to be managerialy prudent, perhaps. But holding back on charging costs when things are not quite so buoyant might be less benignly looked upon.

Currency valuation

This can be manipulated slightly if there are a sufficient number of transactions and if a large number of currencies are used, simply by changing dates slightly for when transactions are recorded. The scope for this has in one direction become more limited with the growth of electronic trading in currencies done by companies themselves (instantaneous exchange and with electronic audit trails) but at the same time this has also allowed more latitude for companies to choose the date at which they effect exchanges of currency.

The balance sheet

This is really where most of the distortion usually occurs. Stocks are the prime area for some form of adjustment.

Valuing stocks is as much a matter of judgement as of science – particularly when some form of part-processing has occurred. The inclusion of overheads (see above) is one of the more sophisticated problems. Simply identifying stocks can be a troublesome business in large companies – even those which have no intention of producing anything but squeaky-clean accounts.

In times of financial turmoil, in rapid-moving markets or where no standard third-party benchmark exists, these problems become very complicated. In the 1970s, for instance, the innocent problem of valuing stocks in a time of high inflation gave rise to massive contortions on the part of the accounting profession as they dealt with (honest) stock valuations: LIFO and FIFO accounting (Last In First Out; First In First Out) are almost diametrically opposed in terms of their operational chronology to manufacturing processes (most processes would hold that oldest stock should be used first) but the use of FIFO accounting in a time of high inflation could lead to the collapse of a company's profits, cash flows and operations, as the company's accounting practices failed to reflect the true cost of replacing raw materials. This then allowed a good deal of potential jiggery-pokery, too, in assessing how much stocks were truly worth.

Valuing *tangible assets* is also a fraught area even in times of stable economic conditions – especially when those assets are subject to depreciation. The life over which an asset has manufacturing or operational value can again be something of a judgemental issue and it is certain that not all productive assets are scrapped at the end of their accounting lives, as a rigorous application of the concept of depreciation would require.

The valuation of *intangible assets* – brand-names; 'goodwill'; intellectual property – has become a subject of some difficulty for accounting concepts. Consequently, problems are always thrown up about how these should be reflected in the accounts and where this occurs there is room for the unscrupulous to exercise their bent for deception.

When two companies join together after a merger or an acquisition, great scope arises for an imaginative application of *accounting conventions* in valuing assets and accounting for overhead costs. And if the accounting policies of the two companies are not quite congruent, then the scope for 'judgement' is even wider.

Not all of these occurrences are malign, of course. Accountants and managers have to wrestle with conceptual problems all the time in trying to ascribe values and sometimes they will disagree. Sometimes they will make errors in good faith which have to be corrected later in the light of better information. Sometimes they might make perfectly acceptable decisions, which later, better information renders incorrect. But sometimes some managers use the fog of insufficient scrutiny to make decisions which are good only for them.

As far as the investor or analyst is concerned, it is rarely possible to detect such mischief in one set of accounts. If it is, then the perpetrator is singularly incompetent and should find a new line of criminality. Flaws in the structure of the inventions that have to be made are usually only detectable after a run of two or three sets of accounts, as the stretched 'truth' gets more and more difficult to hold together.

Even so, sometimes with the collusion of the company's professional advisers – or varying degrees of incompetence – it is possible for these frauds to run and run. It is not very often that 'amateur' investors are able to discern the truth – rarely are amateurs able to marshal the resources to track and analyse what the professionals have taken pains to conceal. Not until someone decides to blow the whistle on the affair from the inside – as in the case of the Enron collapse – does the truth begin to come out.

CHAPTER 14

Mischief – the practice

AUDIT PROBLEMS

The failure of Enron illustrates one of the reasons why companies hold on to their audit relationships for so long. A change of auditor often brings about the revelation of some scam or other, as the incoming auditors display marginally more enterprise or professional competence or less simple naivety than their predecessors in looking at the company's books for the first time.

This is why accounting scams are often uncovered on a change of control – and it is also the justification for the new, incoming managers to take a highly cynical view of the past earnings record of the acquired company – criticising all the dubious accounting practices of their predecessors that they, of course, would *never* indulge in – in order to help inflate their own (future) record.

Enron

Enron is the one case in corporate fraud that everyone has probably heard about. It was a manifestation of events that had been happening – unrecognised except by a few – for several decades. When it collapsed in 2001 it was (until then) the largest bankruptcy in US corporate history, taking with it 20,000 jobs (from its own staff) and later the staff of its auditors Arthur Andersen, to say nothing of possibly thousands from less-significant suppliers. The company had claimed revenues the previous year (2000) of $111 billion.

Background

Enron grew out of the amalgamation of (individually honest) oil and gas companies based in the southeast of the USA into a business which created, developed and controlled markets rather than physical product.

Under the pretence of advancing shareholder wealth, Enron's senior managers developed policies and products that effectively destroyed the well-being and economic prospects of millions of people worldwide. Domestically, with political complicity (sometimes bought, sometimes merely ideologically based) previously well-regulated markets for energy were disrupted and distorted. Internationally, rational investment in power generation in Third World countries was subverted.

By the time it collapsed, Enron was a procedurally corrupt company. From the concealment of loans (via the 'raptor' companies which are examined more fully below), through the options-based 'incentivisation' of managers and the symbiotic relationship of the auditors Arthur Andersen, to the destruction of information and propagation of lies over its trading patterns, it employed every piece of accounting trickery it could and developed some that had never been seen before in the accounts of supposedly highly regulated public companies.

Enron's senior management were crooked – and some of them were jailed for their crimes. Their actions were devoted entirely to their own enrichment with shareholders' interests completely disregarded. To this end the accounts of the company were completely unreliable after an odyssey of concealment, truth-warping and falsification.

However, such concealment and distortion could not have been achieved without the active collusion of the company's lawyers, auditors and bankers and the somnolence of the company's non-executive directors.

The Raptors – Enron's own Jurassic Park

The so-called 'raptor' structures that Enron employed – a rather geeky name for the off-balance sheet entities – were not simple off-the-shelf affairs but were highly complex corporate arrangements. They should have been tracked, traced and verified by bankers and lawyers who were paid not simply to follow the company's interest but also to protect those of the public. These advisers were, instead, more concerned with accelerating fees than with observing the (admittedly malleable) ethical codes of their own professions. The non-executive directors of the company – among them one dean of accounting from an 'Ivy League' business school – were simply completely derelict in their duties.

A few brave souls among the ranks of analysts and brokers pointed out that the emperor had no clothes – and were usually punished commercially for doing so by being excluded by Enron from its constant round of debt and equity issues – until the whistleblower surfaced. But by and large broking houses, major banks and the media allowed themselves to be intimidated or sold their integrity for a flow of fees or access to sensitive market information.

Where the domestically regulated markets didn't suit them, Enron's managers lobbied politicians for change. If the consequences of those changes were still not to the maximum advantage of the company, Enron's managers distorted accounting rules and governance procedures to tip the balance in their favour.

How then did they get away with it for so long?

Apart from the bullying of stock-broking analysts and bankers – and the knowing collusion of the group's lawyers and auditors – Enron's senior managers employed two main accounting devices to continue to hoodwink the market.

The regulatory basis of the frauds

The first of these was the use of '*off-balance sheet*' *accounting* to conceal its inherent financial weakness.

In essence, the company loaded related companies (but not subsidiaries or associates) with debt. Using these it was able to keep all the debt off its own balance sheet so appearing to be far stronger than it really was. It kept track of these by having a senior director – the finance director, Andy Fastow – as its nominee on these companies. (Fastow signed agreements with Enron to cement the ownership details.)

These companies (which grew rapidly in number as the company's needs for concealment increased) were the so-called 'Raptor' or SPE (Special Purpose Entity) companies. They were named sequentially – Raptor I; Raptor II; and so on. (Raptors are a class of predatory birds that hunt and feed on other animals and have their origins in the fearsome dinosaurs of the Jurassic era.)

The second method was to adopt a weak piece of accounting regulation called '*mark-to-market*' *accounting* and use it in a pernicious fashion. (The rules are contained in the American Federal Accounting Standard 115 and this has the status of a Generally Accepted Accounting Principle, or GAAP, used worldwide in consequence.)

The flaw in FRS 115 went to the root of the purpose of company accounts. The *raison d'être* of accountants is to measure financial quantities to produce values that can be used in compiling Profit and Loss accounts and balance sheets. This obligation, as they see it, to ascribe a value to everything, means that where no measurement device exists, they will feel compelled to invent one.

However this fixation sometimes leads them into a Wonderland world where quantities are defined purely in terms of themselves and leads into the surreal realm where the number one truly can be a liar and two and two can be proven to make five.

'Mark-to-market accounting' has the same effect in accounting and ascribing values as did Humpty Dumpty's phrase in Alice's *Through the Looking Glass* when he told her that:

'. . . *words mean whatever I choose them to mean. Neither more nor less.*'

Alice went on to reply:

'*The question is, whether you can make words mean so many different things.*'

'*The question is,*' said Humpty Dumpty, '*which is to be master – that's all.*'

In encapsulating the ethics of Enron, the exchange might have been written by Fastow – or by Jeffery Skilling, the chief exec, or Kenneth Lay, the chairman of Enron.

The principal problem arises because FAS115 requires finance directors and auditors to attribute a value to an intangible entity by reference to its market value. This is used for identifying asset values to go into balance sheets or in calculating the profit or loss that flows from income streams from those entities. This *sometimes* works when there is a valid marketplace. In the case of Enron, because they were at the same time describing, creating and developing these markets where none had previously existed – and so there was no neutral reference point – it gave maximum latitude for virtually unlimited financial wickedness. In the pursuit of their own best interests, the senior managers of the company took full use of such latitude.

Unfortunately, because of the circumstances under which Enron was operating, investors were all too willing to dispense with the normally accepted principles of physics and chemistry and were quite prepared to be gulled into accepting that the company could conjure money and markets out of nothing, and that what went up did not have to come down at some time. The underlying precept of the promoters of the South Sea Bubble comes to mind again – 'an undertaking of Great Advantage but no one to know what it is'.

The lessons to be learned for analysis

There are no accounting methods for an outsider to prove that such malign practices are taking place if the managers of the company, its auditors and its lawyers all collude to defraud – as they did with Enron.

Eventually a very few professional fund managers broke away from the pack mentality that had driven the share price up and began to question the company's finances. They were turning their backs on what appeared to be a sure-fire winner for their funds when they did so and were consequently treated to a good deal of adverse comment and derision.

But Enron's profit record looked too good to be true – and the first rule of investing is 'If it looks too good to be true – then it probably is.' In this case, despite the inability of critics to produce conclusive evidence of fraud until the whistle was blown, the natural connections that ought to have existed between the various parts of the accounts were not there. This ought to have provided warning enough.

Parmalat
The background

Parmalat was originally a small dairy business based around the agricultural industry of the northern Italian city of Parma. It was started by the company's founder, Calisto (Carlo) Tanzi in 1961 after he dropped out of his university course.

After thirty years of modest growth, the company listed on the Milan Stock Exchange in 1991; the board had long been dominated by friends of Tanzi and by family members and after the flotation the family retained control, which should have been a warning to outsiders.

In the years after the listing, the company began steadily to acquire new businesses. The group rapidly became a substantial national, then European and finally global dairy products business, taking advantage of de-regulation in the dairy market in Italy (and Europe) and the break up of the state monopoly under Silvio Berlusconi. While the state monopoly effectively became a private monopoly under Tanzi, Parmalat was never pursued or interfered with by the Italian authorities.

The group's expansion was funded by bonds (which were not as risky as debt for the banks) and Parmalat's directors made sure that all the Italian merchant banks were involved in the raising of the money through bond sales channelled through the banks. The major ratings agencies never questioned the credit-worthiness of Parmalat or of individual debt instruments.

However, in 2003 a 'surprise' bond issue of 500 million euros – surprise because it was announced the then FD, Fausto Tonna, without the apparent knowledge of Tanzi – resulted in Tonna's dismissal. The new FD found he had no access to some of the accounting records, which were under the control of the chief accountant and began to make inquiries into the true state of the group's balance sheet.

When the new FD was dismissed soon after taking up his post (presumably for getting too close to the truth) and replaced by the chief accountant, the market began to get nervous and the share price steadily declined.

The Parmalat group collapsed on Christmas Eve 2003 with total debts of €14.3 billion. It transpired that the accounts had been falsified for at least 10 years previously.

The basis of the fraud

The group had used similar bullying tactics to Enron in that company's approach to analysts and banks, making sure that anyone critical of the company was excluded from the lucrative bond-raising business. No analysts had questioned the higher margins than competitors that Parmalat was able to achieve. No one ever asked the question about how while turnover slipped, profits continued to increase.

It was not until days before the collapse that one broker – Smith Barney – issued an analysts' report which said:

> '. . . *our inability to reconcile the operating cash flow with the reduction of net debt has yet to be fully explained to our satisfaction by the company.*'

Much of the money which should have been in the company had been siphoned off to an offshore vehicle called the Epicurum fund. The Greek philosopher Epicurus was much concerned with developing the principles of a living a life without pain or suffering – so the name of the fund is a little – very little – joke.

Grant Thornton – the auditors to whom the audit was sub-contracted by Deloitte & Touche when the company decided to change its main auditors – had signed off accounts on the basis of a forged document – *which they never independently verified.* These documents, which were crude forgeries, purported to show investments in the Epicurum fund matching the debt obligations of the company.

Much of the money has never been traced. It is almost certain that Parmalat was a laundry business rather than a dairy business.

The Tesco 'support payments' affair

Brief reference should also be made – lest British readers think that scandals are solely a foreign problem – to the misbehaviour of Tesco in the UK, which was revealed in 2014. But since this case is being actively investigated at the time of writing, the scope for comment is necessarily limited.

It is common practice among supermarkets and large retail chains in the UK to ask their suppliers for 'support payments'. These can be for anything that the retailer can get away with – from putting products on shelves where customers are more likely to see them, to running promotional campaigns favouring one brand over another, to assistance with ensuring shelves are kept completely stacked – even to retrospective discounts on costs. As the practice has grown across the sector, so the volumes of money involved have also grown.

What appears to have happened in Tesco's case is that the company's practice of dunning its suppliers for fees to either push their products against competitors, or to help with display and stacking 'costs', or to underwrite volume discounts, gradually began to get misused. In particular, the timing of the matching of the suppliers fees began to get seriously out of kilter with the sales that they were supposed to support – so much so and in such large amounts that they began to be viewed as a profit stream in their own right.

The company must have become increasingly threatened by the incursions into its market of European supermarket chains during the early 2000s. These European chains operated to different business models and so perhaps Tesco thought, in the absence of competing on price, it could ill afford (in its own estimation) to release any chance to secure income to bolster its earning record and dominance of the sector.

What appears to have happened is that this eventually led to the company reporting profits that were not 'real' but were based on substantial anticipated support from payments from suppliers. They were anticipated in the sense that though they may have been received they were not in accordance with the obligation to match expenditure against income nor were they prudently accounted for.

The scale of this over-recording seems to be substantial and amounts to hundreds of millions of pounds over a period of many years. The company appears to have been mis-stating its publicly reported profits over this period.

This looks like not so much a deliberate accounting scandal designed to mislead, as much as a managerial policy, with its basis in permitted accounting and managerial behaviour, which gradually moved out of control. But exactly where one ends and another begins is often very difficult to disentangle.

The Sino-Forest Affair

There is no such haziness about the policies in respect of Sino-Forest.

Stock exchanges

As a preamble to this story, one thing that every investor should be aware of is that not all stock exchanges operate to the same level of supervision or regulation. While they may be efficient in terms of matching buyers and sellers of shares and making sure that settlements occur properly, the supervision of their member companies can be very different.

The Toronto Exchange, in particular, has long been run in such a way as allow its critics to call it a Wild West market. This makes it attractive to companies that do not wish to have a high level of 'intrusive' regulation into their businesses, since the costs of regulation are borne by these companies through their fees to the exchange. Less regulation means lower fees.

Critics maintain that the lower level of regulation means that investors know less about the companies which are listed and that this can lead to dubious practices and the occasional scandal, as the unscrupulous use the free manoeuvring room available in lax regulatory practices to bilk the dupes.

The Sino-Forest debacle did nothing to lessen their criticisms and much to validate them.

Background

The facts of the case are these. Sino-Forest was a timber products company whose arboricultural assets were based on mainland China. It listed on the Alberta exchange through a reverse takeover of a dormant shell company in 1994. It moved to the Toronto Stock Exchange in 1995, with a chairman and supervisory board who were chosen to lend some supposed gravitas to the business rather than for their intimate knowledge of its operations . . . the words of the South Sea Company prospectus seem to come back yet again.

The company was originally set up by a Chinese 'entrepreneur', Alan Chan, with the collaboration of a division of the state-owned timber products company to produce micro-density fibre boards from timber plantations close to the city of Zhanjiang in China's Guangdong province. Demand for wood for building was rising quickly as China's growing economy grew rapidly.

The company founder's early business ventures had nothing to do with trees. At the age of twenty-eight, he took a job as corporate secretary for the notorious Hong Kong harbour tourist trap called the 'Jumbo Floating Restaurant'. His attempt to purchase a ship-building business in 1988 ended with Chan accused of misappropriating funds. He later wrote a financial column for the *Hong Kong Economic Journal* and authored business books under the name Koon Chung-lin, which is how he apparently came to the attention of the manager of the state timber plantations.

None of these facts appeared in the prospectus for the company on its listing on either of the Canadian exchanges. Yet Chan had targeted Canadian investors particularly because of their supposed familiarity with timber products companies.

For more than a decade and a half, Sino-Forest appeared to be a stupendous success story. Between 1994 and 1997, it reported $60 million (US) in sales. Buying, managing and selling trees and forestry assets in mainland China, the firm's profit increased from $3 million in 1994 to $395.4 million in 2010.

The basis of the fraud

Unfortunately, the Leizhou joint venture never produced a single panel, according to a key executive involved in the project who gave a statement to the Toronto *Globe and Mail* newspaper (which he later retracted), after the company received a highly negative investment evaluation from Muddy Waters Research, an independent research firm (and 'short-seller' of the company's shares).

All the while it had apparently been falsifying its accounts and camouflaging and obscuring the true picture with inter-company transactions. Sino-Forest relied on a complex financial structure in which most of its timber assets were bought, sold and held through wholly owned subsidiaries located in the British Virgin Islands.

Transactions at those subsidiaries were not properly recorded and were difficult to track or independently audit, so that the auditors, Ernst & Young, could not independently confirm the cash flows had happened or that the revenue was properly recognised because of the way the BVI entities operated.

Sino-Forest was spending the money it raised from Canadian investors (read 'speculators') on undeclared 'related-party' transactions – buying (supposed) assets from people who were associated with the firm and consequently whose commercial relationships should have been made known to other investors.

How it lasted . . . And how it was found out

The scam could be disguised for so long because (a) it was extremely difficult to pierce the smokescreen of misinformation; (b) insufficient attention was paid to supervising the information that was released to investors by regulators; and (c) the company's Canadian board were insufficiently concerned to find out what was going on, being quite happy to bask in their association with a fast-growing company and take the appropriate fees for so doing.

It was discovered because every company that experiences such a rapid rise attracts the interest of 'short-sellers' who are willing to bet that the share price is inflated and will 'correct' (that is, collapse at some point). This then offers them an opportunity to sell shares they do not actually own (some institutions will 'lend' shares for this purpose) – to those who are keen to accept the herd wisdom and buy the stock, in the expectation that they can buy them back at a lower price before their selling deal becomes 'live' and requires settlement to actually physically complete the bargain.

But these short-sellers have to do a lot of homework to justify their speculation. The focus of their investigations is from a highly critical attitude towards the reports of the company – whereas investors who have a preference for making an investment may well approach information more sympathetically. Muddy Waters Research is just such a critically focused research house.

Muddy Waters claimed to have spent two man-years investigating the company before it published its research – aware that it might well be the target of hostile counter-punches from those investors who had bought in to the company's story. One such investor was John Paulson, who lost about $100m on his investment in Sino-Forest. (Don't feel too sorry for him – Paulson is the investor who infamously assisted Goldman Sachs create a 'doomed-to-fail investment' for banks just before the 2007 financial crisis and then proceeded to bet against it in the secure knowledge he would be correct, since he had helped devise it).

What tipped Muddy Waters off to the whole sorry affair was that S-F was generating vast profits but never paid a dividend and was unable to prove it was cash-rich (despite its verbal claims). The lack of cash was counter-intuitive to the company's record – as was the constant need to draw new cash from investors, if profits and revenue generation were so good.

Presumably any clued-up, diligent and very resolute investor with two man-years to spare, lots of cash to support the investigations and good contacts in the timber industry and in China could have done the same!

CHAPTER 15

Summary – the lessons to be drawn

Insight

Comparing information

Complete use of the accounts

Knowing what to compare

The importance of checking

Completeness

This final chapter draws together some of the significant points from previous chapters to emphasise some major issues that should be borne in mind while analysing and particularly interpreting accounts. This is not supposed to be a comprehensive checklist of issues that have to be thought of – it is a reinforcement of issues of technique that should be constantly in mind when looking at accounts.

INSIGHT

The mechanical issues of dismembering each of the major three sections of the accounts are fairly straightforward. Once the concepts of what accounts represent have been absorbed, then comparing them and contrasting them to give additional information or to remove obscurity becomes a simple matter of manipulation of data. Practice at this makes perfect – or at least competent and confident.

But what the analyst is always seeking is the alchemist's stone of insight that transforms *data* into *information*. The accounts are full of data, in the form of numbers that have been carefully compiled from raw records and then re-configured, according to accounting principles, to provide a sort of portal into understanding the company and its activities. Each individual entry in the published accounts is a composite value derived from hundreds – perhaps thousands – of others. Some of those will be themselves summary values from groupings of additional thousands. At the level at which the analyst approaches them these numbers are just data which have to be leavened with some imagination to fully understand and interpret what is going on. Through this, data – the blunt instrument– is converted into information – the sharp point which can be focused.

At the level of abstraction of company accounts, numbers are little more than ciphers in a code about the company that can only be unlocked by applying some form of insight. The portal that the number represents – a door – can be unlocked by applying some insight into what the raw material of the numbers can convey when sharpened and focused.

This is best gained from outside the company, comparing and contrasting the subject company with similar ones – either with those in the same sector or those with similar financial characteristics from different sectors.

This takes both practice and diligence. It is necessary to have some feeling for the economics of sectors to be able to make reasoned evaluations of company behaviour and the pressures on companies —and this only comes with some application of time and trouble to investigate the pressures, through reading and observing.

While it is perfectly reasonable to anticipate that a first-timer can produce a reasoned investigation of a set of company accounts, it is unrealistic to expect a *series* of accurate forecasts of company's profits that is held together by anything more than luck, from the same individual. Gathering together the wherewithal to make accurate reasoned forecasts is an investment in itself – as already noted, in time and information-gathering.

COMPARING INFORMATION

The second crucial factor has already been touched on. The analyst should always be comparing information. Pieces of information gathered internally in the accounts should be viewed in the context of other information from the same source to see how the jigsaw fits together.

Information from one set of accounts should also be compared with similar pieces of information gathered historically over a run of years to establish trends in the way a company's accounts move in response to economic or managerial action.

Information from one company should also be compared with similar pieces from other companies. This comes again to the issue of generating the focus of insight and being aware of what is important in looking at a company – which pieces of information may be crucial to understanding and which may be superfluous; which may seem significant but are of minor importance; which are hiding their significance that will only be fully revealed with the addition of some other piece of information from somewhere else in the accounts.

COMPLETE USE OF THE ACCOUNTS

It is not very much of an exaggeration to say that every page in a set of accounts will provide a piece of information that will help unlock the code. Each page certainly will contribute something to the jigsaw.

That means that no page can be disregarded. After a brief initial reconnaissance of every page in a report and accounts set, scrutinising each page diligently will help to establish a mental picture of the company that can be built on using snippets and blocks of information from all the other pages.

To do this properly requires the analyst to hold information in the memory – not necessarily consciously but certainly in such a way that a discordant piece of information or something that adds to the synthesis of additional piece of information can be automatically recalled and utilised. This is both a trick that some people can cultivate and an intuitive process that some people do naturally. If you are one of the lucky ones, then the process of investigation and analysis becomes much easier. If not, invest in a good notebook and record your thoughts as you go along.

KNOWING WHAT TO COMPARE

Looking at the mass of information in a set of accounts for the first time is a bit like looking at a darkened room having just come from a brightly lit one. Dark hulks of information are evident but how they fit into the overall shape of the room takes time to work out. Knowing how to look at a set of accounts – what to look at first; what corroborates and what leads into further investigations; what is of secondary importance and what is a lead factor – is an important skill to develop.

It is particularly important to grasp early on, to enable accurate forecasting, the significance and power of the 'equivalent half' method. A sequential analysis of a company's results will probably produce a misleading result. Most companies have definite stronger and weaker half years. Basing a forecasting on a strictly sequential, but usually inaccurate, analysis – H1 to H2; H1 to H2 rather than the leap-frog process of H1 to H1 and then H2 to H2 then the full year – will distort the resulting effort and leave the inexperienced analyst wondering what could possibly have been missed to push the predicted result so far away from what was eventually reported.

By contrast, though it may seem counter-intuitive, much stronger – and more accurate predictions – can be made by harnessing the bias of the half-year to temper runs of predicted data with the likely characteristics of a company's trading patterns.

Some companies will always surprise with unexpected movements in their trading patterns but the number which does not have some form of more-or-less predictable half-year bias is very small.

THE IMPORTANCE OF CHECKING

In handling lots of data it is very easy to makes mistakes – transliteration errors, transcription errors and skipping errors are probably the most common. When faults like these are made during the process of forecasting, a great deal of careful analysis can be rendered worthless by one simple error.

A recollection

When I was learning the skills of analysis, the head of research of the company I worked for accompanied me on a company visit to discuss a company's prospects. I had stayed up very late the previous night to complete a forecast, very conscious of the importance of this first visit on which he had come to see how well I was doing. The company was a complicated one with lots of different subsidiaries and market sectors. I had completed my forecast only early in the morning in consequence, wrestling with putting numbers from different spreadsheets into one master forecast (this was so long ago it was before the common use of laptop computers). I had been tired and made a transliteration error in the estimate of future interest charges, which although it only affected the outcome slightly, stood out like a sore thumb when you looked at it with fresh eyes.

The head of research made it plain, without any trace of sympathy (he was a humourless man) as we walked away from the company's premises, that he regarded my lapse as having absolutely jeopardised the good name of the firm for several decades hence – not just with this one company but probably with the entire London share market. I considered my fate with the company sealed. (I was only saved by the fact that when the company did report its financial year results, my forecast had proved to be an almost-flawless estimate of future profitability notwithstanding the error because of the disguising effects of large numbers.) But I did not make the same mistake again – because I developed my own methods of checking and my own procedures for making sure I did not miss a crucial piece of information.

(Years later I confess that I felt a shudder of pleasure when the former head of research was found guilty of a serious lapse of administration and fined a very large amount of money for having neglected to accurately complete a simple declaration to the regulating authorities.)

There are a number of devices that can be used to reduce the potential damage of these pitfalls. Written checklists, simultaneous entry of information, linked spreadsheets (if they are used) can all play their part. Most involve merely appropriate care and simple procedures individuals will develop for themselves.

But the lesson of the episode I went through and what I learned from it, is the importance of checking all the time that the information being put down line-by-line makes sense – and that the overall result makes sense too. And don't just check for arithmetical accuracy – check for logical sense too, in the sub-lines of the forecast. So, for instance, if the level of debt rises over a year, then all other things being equal, interest charges will rise too. Or if the industry margins are under pressure, make sure that the final forecast for the year is similarly adjusted.

Check, check and then check again. To paraphrase what the head of research obviously thought – the meeting wasn't a matter of life and death. It was much more important that that.

COMPLETENESS

A sub-set of the need for checking is to make sure that all necessary issues have been dealt with. Don't adjust the margins but forget to look at the cash generation, for instance. Or don't include the effects of an acquisition but then forget to increase debt consequentially, taking into account the combined company totals and not just the historical trend of the acquiring company.

In time, completing a forecast will involve a set of procedures that become almost second nature. What needed initially an inordinate degree of attention to process (which can almost threaten the need to think about the reasons *behind* the process) will become routine. This in itself may begin to pose a threat to effective forecasting as the process becomes automatic and original and fresh thinking suffers.

Each new analysis, and forecast, should really be started as if it were for the first time, adapting the tricks and techniques learned from previous times to each new opportunity.

That is what provides some of the satisfaction to properly understanding and interpreting company accounts – being able to take them apart piece by piece and then knowing how to build them up again for the purpose of making predictions of profitability.

Making forecasts which turn out to be correct – because the jigsaw puzzle was properly understood – can have an intellectual satisfaction – as well as saving you from blowing the family legacy on a sure-fire investment proposal that turns out to be a Parmalat, or an Enron, or a Sino-Forest.

UK accounting and corporate scandals 2000 to 2015 – a list of the major scandals

John Ho Park (1999; Griffin Trading; London)
Equitable Life (2000)

Administration of Turner and Newall (2001)

Qinetiq privatisation (2002) – civil servants both negotiated and benefitted from privatisation

Royal Dutch Shell reserves restatement (2004) – extensive misleading statements

Actis Capital and CDC (2004) – excessive remuneration

Langbar International (2005)

BP Texas City blast (2005) – cost-cutting reduces maintenance and causes explosion

BAe ethics report (Woolf Report – 2008) – Al-Yamama

RBS/ABN Amro (2007) – uninvestigated acquisition that precipitated bank collapse

Northern Rock failure (2008) – the start of the 2007–8 financial crisis

Sirbir (2009) – mismanagement of a public company

Carphone Warehouse (2009) – directors' loans

JJB Loans scandal (2009) – directors' loans

Keydata (2009) – improper accounting

Farepak (2009) – loss of Christmas savings funds

The Phoenix 4 – Leyland (2009) – preferential terms for directors

Arch Cru failure (2009) – investment fund fraud; subsequent mismanagement by administrators

Mitchells and Butler (2009) – financial engineering that lost shareholders £¼bn

Weavering Capital (2009) – hedge fund failure brought about by fraud

The PPI Scandals (all UK banks – continuing restitution)

LIBOR manipulation (all UK banks – continuing investigation)

FOREX manipulation (all UK banks – continuing investigation)

Money laundering (several UK Banks but especially HSBC and Standard Chartered)

The Volkswagen emission test falsification

Audit failures, an incomplete list, worldwide over the last thirty years

ZZZZ Best; 1986; Ernst & Whinney; United States. Ponzi scheme run by Barry Minkow

Barlow Clowes; 1988; Deloitte; United Kingdom. Fraud and theft

MiniScribe; 1989; Coopers & Lybrand; United States. False invoicing

Bank of Credit and Commerce International; 1991; PricewaterhouseCoopers/Ernst & Whinney; United Kingdom. Violation of lending laws and money laundering

Phar-Mor; 1992; Coopers & Lybrand; United States mail fraud, wire fraud, bank fraud, and transportation of funds obtained by theft or fraud; losses estimated at $1bn

Informix Corporation; 1996; Ernst & Young; United States. Massively overstated revenue

Wickes; 1996; Arthur Andersen; UK; losses concealed

Sybase; 1997; Ernst & Young; United States. Artificially inflated profits using side letters

Cendant; 1998; Ernst & Young; United States. False business statements over several years, wiping $14 billion off market value

Waste Management, Inc.; 1999; Arthur Andersen; United States. Financial mis-statements

MicroStrategy; 2000; PricewaterhouseCoopers; United States. Mis-statement of results and fraud

Unify Corporation; 2000; Deloitte & Touche; United States. Inflated revenue statements 'Round tripping' – supplying funds to customers for them to buy products with no expectation of the funds being repaid

Computer Associates; 2000; KPMG; United States. Massive frauds to inflate share price

Xerox; 2000; KPMG; United States. Falsifying financial results

One.Tel; 2001; Ernst & Young; Australia

Enron; 2001; Arthur Andersen; United States. See page 132

Adelphia; 2002; Deloitte & Touche; United States. Milking of company funds by founders

AOL; 2002; Ernst & Young; United States. Inflated sales

Bristol-Myers Squibb; 2002; PricewaterhouseCoopers; United States. Inflated sales

CMS Energy; 2002; Arthur Andersen; United States. 'Round trip' trades

Duke Energy; 2002; Deloitte & Touche; United States. 'Round trip' trades

Dynegy; 2002; Arthur Andersen; United States. 'Round trip' trades

El Paso Corporation; 2002; Deloitte & Touche; United States. 'Round trip' trades

Freddie Mac; 2002; PricewaterhouseCoopers; United States. Understated earnings

Global Crossing; 2002; Arthur Andersen; Bermuda. Network capacity swaps to inflate revenues

Halliburton; 2002; Arthur Andersen; United States. Improper booking of cost overruns

Homestore.com; 2002; PricewaterhouseCoopers; United States. Improper booking of sales

Kmart; 2002; PricewaterhouseCoopers; United States. Misleading accounting practices

Mirant; 2002; KPMG; United States. Overstated assets and liabilities

Nicor; 2002; Arthur Andersen; United States. Overstated assets, understated liabilities

Peregrine Systems; 2002; KPMG; United States. Overstated sales

Qwest Communications; 1999, 2000, 2001, 2002; Arthur Andersen; 2002 October KPMG. United States. Inflated revenues

Reliant Energy; 2002; Deloitte & Touche; United States. 'Round trip' trades

Sunbeam; 2002; Arthur Andersen; United States

Tyco International; 2002; PricewaterhouseCoopers; Bermuda. Improper accounting

WorldCom; 2002; Arthur Andersen; United States. Overstated cash flows

Royal Ahold; 2003; Deloitte & Touche; United States. Inflating promotional allowances

Parmalat; 2003; Grant Thornton Spa; Italy. Falsified accounting documents

HealthSouth Corporation; 2003; Ernst & Young; United States. Exaggerated earnings

Chiquita Brands International; 2004;Ernst & Young United States. Illegal payments

AIG; 2004; PricewaterhouseCoopers; United States. Accounting of structured financial deals unremarked or queried

MG Rover; 2005; Deloittes; UK. Deliberate disregard of professional ethics

BAe; 1997–2007; KPMG; audit failure in respect of bribes and concealment of subsidiaries; case dropped by FRC as outdated

Bernard L. Madoff Investment Securities LLC; 2008; Friehling & Horowitz; United States. Ponzi scheme

Anglo Irish Bank; 2008; Ernst & Young; Ireland. Hidden loans controversy

Satyam Computer Services; 2009; PricewaterhouseCoopers; India. Falsified accounts

Cattles plc; 2009 PwC; KPMG; Deloittes; UK. Creditors mounting action for recovery of £1.6bn

Lehman Brothers; 2010; Ernst & Young; United States. Failure to disclose Repo 105 transactions to investors

Sino-Forest Corporation; 2011; Ernst & Young; Canada-China. Asset loss or non-existence

Olympus Corporation; 2011; Ernst & Young; Japan. 'Tobashi' frauds using acquisitions

Autonomy Corporation; 2012; Deloitte & Touche; United States. Accounting uncertainty in acquisition

Quinn Insurance; 2010; PriceWaterhouseCoopers; Ireland. Case pending – possible breaches of solvency rules

Vincent Tchenguiz (via the SFO) 2012; Grant Thornton; UK. Excerpt from judge's comments: ' . . . Its conduct has repeatedly crossed the line from proper ethical practice into areas of ethical, civil and potentially criminal wrongdoing . . . '

. . . And so on . . . and so on . . . and so on . . .

Further Reading

For those who might like to extend their knowledge, there are several books which deal with the way that the City works or document specific accounting scandals or look at the theory of accounting scams.

The Money Machine (by Philip Coggan; published by Penguin revised 2009) provides a very approachable explanation of the way that the mechanisms of the City operate. *The Death of Gentlemanly Capitalism* (by Philip Augar; also published by Penguin, 2000) goes on to look more critically at the way that the City has changed in the thirty years since the last major organisational upheaval (the 1986 Financial Services Act).

The scandal that almost everyone has heard of is the Enron debacle from 2000. Several good books have been written about this – *Enron: The Anatomy of Greed* (Brian Cruver; Arrow, 2002) is probably the best insider's account. The whole affair was first documented by Bethany McLean, in her book *The Smartest Guys in the Room* (Penguin, 2003), which was also made into a film.

For inexplicable reasons, British corporate scandals tend to attract less ink and paper than they once did. A recent exception would be the collapse of the major UK banks, where a flurry of titles have appeared in the past couple of years – among them *Shredded* (by Ian Fraser; published by Birlinn, 2013) and *Black Horse Ride* (Ivan Fallon; The Robson Press, 2015). The apogee of reporting on corporate scandals was reached in the later part of the last century and assiduous readers will finds tens of titles dealing with the likes of crooks and scoundrels whose names have largely been forgotten except by students of the scam – Bernie Cornfeld; Emil Savundra; Barlow Clowes; Lord and Lady Docker; John de Lorean; Robert Maxwell, to identify just a handful. Their names may now be unfamiliar but the techniques of deception they employed often live on.

More academic (and slightly patchy in style) but exemplary in its coverage is *Creative Accounting: Fraud and Corporate Accounting Scandals* (edited by Michael Jones; published by Wiley, 2010) which looks at the plethora of scandals and techniques employed worldwide to conceal, disguise, trick and steal money from investors.

Last, for those who might like to look at the wider techniques supposed to counter the culture and circumstances that give rise to accounting fraud inside organizations, the coverage (and shortcomings) of corporate governance is dealt with in my book *Theory and Practice of Corporate Governance* (Cambridge University Press, 2013).

Some additional explanations – company status – and two definitions

The following explanations of terms may help those who have not dealt with the legal status of companies before.

There are three main methods of conducting trading:

1. *Sole trader* – an individual who is solely responsible for the liabilities of the business he is engaged in and who also owns the assets of the business. The business may employ others and can be identified '& Co' since this does not imply an 'incorporated status' but only indicates that other people are also engaged in the common pursuit of the business with the proprietor.

2. *Partnership* – effectively two or more people acting together in pursuit of a commercial aim. Their liability is 'joint and several' – they are responsible for their own debts and also for those incurred by their partners, during the course of trading. Professional firms adopted this structure (and were obliged to do so by their professional associations) until the advent of the Limited Partnerships Act 2008.

3. *Limited company* – an incorporated business which has its own legal personality, and so can sue and be sued; can enter into contracts in its own name; and can outlive its originators. A limited company can own and dispose of assets by virtue of these characteristics. The majority of

SOME ADDITIONAL EXPLANATIONS – COMPANY STATUS | 159

trading enterprises are of this type since they offer protection to the shareholders – whose liability for the actions of the company is limited to the original value of their shares (hence the company is limited).

Private companies are identified with the designator '*Ltd*' or '*ltd*' and must use this term in all their trading information, on their stationery and websites.

Larger companies may become *public limited companies* – they have to have a larger share capital and more than one shareholder. They are designated 'PLC ' or 'plc' and again must use this designation (and use it consistently). Companies which reach a certain size are not compelled to become plcs but it would be very difficult to continue to run in the 'ltd' format.

Some *plcs* – but not all – may also have their shares '*listed*' – that is, freely available for sale on a recognised and authorised public exchange. It is these companies which are mostly the subject of this book – although the techniques of analysis are applicable to all companies.

Companies which are owned 100% by a parent company are called (imaginatively) '*wholly owned*' subsidiaries.

Provided a parent owns at least a majority of the issued share capital of another company it is entitled to '*consolidate*' the subsidiary's results. If it owns between 49% and 24% it must account for its proportion of the profits as an 'associated' company. Between 24% and 5% of the company's dividends paid to the parent are to be included in the accounts *as 'minority income'*. Below that level the holding need only be identified as an '*investment*'.

However, although adequate for the purpose of analysis used in this book, this is a highly simplified categorisation. An appropriate legal or accounting textbook should be consulted for more information – especially as to the detail interlinking accounting and ownership obligations.

Two Definitions
Liquid/liquidity
Liquid assets are those that can be easily changed into cash with little or no depletion of value. The most liquid asset of all is, therefore, cash. Liquidity refers to the extent to which a company possesses this quality in its finances.

Gearing – now sometimes called 'leverage'

The extent of a company's balance sheet represented by borrowing. The American term can be misunderstood since it can also apply to the extent to which a company's profits respond to changes in demand (what economists call 'elasticity'). The older English term is consequently preferable but is now in declining usage

Index

The Only Book You Will Ever Need on Branding

Michiel Maandag and Liisa Puolakka

Available to buy in ebook and paperback

This no-nonsense book is for anyone who wants to create a winning brand without drowning in theory.

A great product is not enough. You cannot sell or promote anything without an original and distinctive brand. But how do you create a good name, a memorable logo and a recognizable category so that everyone understands what you are selling?

In *The Only Book You Will Ever Need on Branding* you'll find out everything you need to know – fast.

Using quirky illustrations to make its point you'll discover how to fast forward the success of your brand in a couple of hours. Grasp the key concepts of branding. Learn how to improve your existing brand. Find out what other start-up books don't tell you.

Coaching Skills for Leaders in the Workplace

How to unlock potential and maximise performance

Jackie Arnold

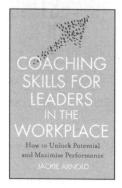

Available to buy in ebook and paperback

This book will give you the knowledge and skills to understand the differences between coaching, supervision and mentoring. It demonstrates how effective coaching programmes can enhance behaviours and retain key staff; reduce recruitment costs; promote well-being and give a robust return on investment.

As a leader, senior manager or executive, you are often called on to act as coach or mentor to your staff. This book will enable you to set up the coaching programmes that will make a significant difference to your organisation. It offers leaders and managers proven behaviours as well as insights into new methods. It also introduces innovative and creative coaching and supervision models and techniques that can be adapted for any environment.

Investing in Stocks and Shares

A step-by-step guide to making money on the stock market

Dr John White

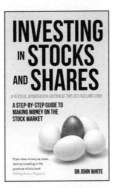

Available to buy in ebook and paperback

A revised, fully updated ninth edition of this bestselling book about investing in stocks and shares

This is one of the most enduring guides to investment in the stock market ever published. Now in a thoroughly revised, updated ninth edition it has been written and kept up to date by a professional long-term investor. It explains in plain English how the stock market works; what affects share prices; how to avoid unnecessary risks; and how you can invest successfully in shares, bonds, gilts, options and futures over the long term.

It gives step-by-step guidance on: how to trade on the stock market, whether it's going up or down; successful stock investment strategies; investing at minimum risk in traded options and futures; buying bonds, gilts and interest-bearing deposits.

Setting Up and Running a Limited Company

A Comprehensive Guide to Forming and Operating a Company as a Director and Shareholder

Robert Browning

Available to buy in ebook and paperback

This practical handbook, now in a thoroughly revised and updated fifth edition with a new chapter on completing your application, will help you understand the mechanics of running a limited company. Whether you have already started your business or are just embarking on it, you will find vital advice on the benefits and obligations of forming a limited company, and how to set one up and run it. There are detailed explanations of the procedures involved, together with essential advice on dealing with statutory information, banking, PAYE, auditing and accounting.

Stand, Speak, Deliver!

How to survive and thrive in public speaking and presenting

Vaughn Evans

Available to buy in ebook and paperback

'There is a real danger that this book will turn public speaking into something that you can actually enjoy.' Graham Davies, speaker and author of *The Presentation Coach*

Public speaking and presenting rank in the top ten of people's greatest fears. Yet being able to speak coherently and persuasively in a speech, seminar or meeting room is important when progressing our careers and living our lives to the fullest.

In this book, 37 short, lively and pithy speeches tell us how to construct and deliver a speech or presentation. Each speech follows a simple, perfect structure which will soon become imprinted in your mind.

Stand, Speak, Deliver! will enable you to learn how to use your eyes, vary your voice and move your body. It will also look at how to inform, entertain, humour, persuade, motivate or inspire the audience; how to present, to colleagues or clients; how to introduce a speaker; and how to wow as best mar

THE
IMPR⟳VEMENT
ZONE

Looking for life inspiration?

The Improvement Zone has it all, from **expert advice** on how to advance your **career** and boost your **business**, to improving your **relationships**, revitalising your **health** and developing your **mind**.

Whatever your goals, head to our website now.

www.improvementzone.co.uk

INSPIRATION ON THE MOVE

INSPIRATION DIRECT TO YOUR INBOX